BRITAIN IN OLD PHOTOGRAPHS

BOLTON WANDERERS

DEAN HAYES

SUTTON PUBLISHING LIMITED

Sutton Publishing Limited
Phoenix Mill · Thrupp · Stroud
Gloucestershire · GL5 2BU

First published 1999

Reprinted in 2002, 2004

British Library Cataloguing in Publication Data
A catalogue record for this book is available from the
British Library.

ISBN 0-7509-2182-X

Typeset in 10/11 Bembo.
Typesetting and origination by
Sutton Publishing Limited.
Printed in Great Britain by
J.H. Haynes & Co. Ltd, Sparkford.

CONTENTS

Nat Lofthouse holds the FA Cup aloft after Bolton's 2–0 victory over Manchester United in the 1958 Final.

INTRODUCTION

Bolton Wanderers began life in 1874 as the Christ Church Sunday School football team. Schoolmaster Thomas Ogden captained the team and the club's president was the local vicar Revd J.F. Wright. Weekly membership was one penny a week, a not insignificant sum in those days. However, when the Vicar of Christ Church tried to put too many restrictions on how church premises could be used, the club broke away and in 1877 formed a new club known as Bolton Wanderers.

They had played their early football at the Park Recreation Ground and Dick Cockle's field but in 1881 they moved home again, this time to Pikes Lane. In those days the club were at the centre of the early intense controversy about professionalism and in 1884 after Preston North End, Burnley and Great Lever had been suspended by the Lancashire FA, Wanderers president Peter Parkinson suggested that a British FA be formed and run independently from the Football Association. As a result, the Wanderers withdrew from the 1884/85 FA Cup competition as both they and their opponents Preston Zingari were embroiled in the issue of professionalism.

In February 1885 J.J. Bentley was appointed secretary of Bolton Wanderers and his knowledge of the game was of great value to the club in the coming months. Despite the club having a successful 1885/86 season, winning the Lancashire Cup, the Bolton Charity Cup and the Derbyshire Charity Cup, off-the-field politics saw Peter Parkinson resign and J.J. Bentley replaced by Billy Struthers. Bentley's administrative skills were sorely missed, however, and in October 1887 he was persuaded to return as the club's secretary.

The Wanderers were founder members of the Football League in 1888 but their early history was relatively undistinguished, although they did finish third in Division One in 1891/92.

Bolton reached the FA Cup Final in 1894 but were beaten 4-1 by Notts County, then a Second Division side at Goodison Park. The Wanderers appeared in a second FA Cup Final in 1904 when they lost 1–0 to Manchester City. The legendary Billy Meredith scored the game's only goal, though it seemed to many to be offside. Bolton were themselves in Division Two by now, but in 1908/09 they won the Second Division Championship, only to be relegated after one season of top flight football. Yet in 1910/11 the Wanderers returned to the First Division as runners-up to West Bromwich Albion.

There is no doubt that the club's golden era was the 1920s and the famous series of three FA Cup Final victories – in 1923, 1926 and 1929. They won the three finals with the help of just 17 players and Pym, Haworth, Seddon and Butler appeared in all three matches. The first of those games was the first final to be staged at the new Wembley Stadium, completed only four days earlier. An estimated 200,000 fans got in to see the Wanderers beat West Ham United 2–0 with goals from David Jack and Joe Smith. In 1926 Bolton went back to Wembley to oppose Manchester City and only an injury to full-back Finney stopped them fielding the side that had beaten West Ham. Bolton won 1–0 thanks to another David Jack goal. The Wanderers made it a hat-trick of wins in 1929, defeating Portsmouth 2–0.

Bolton lost their First Division status in 1932/33 but returned to the top flight after two seasons of Second Division football. The club then entered a period of decline, culminating in the 1946 Burnden Park disaster in which 33 fans died and over 500 were injured. The event overshadowed life at Burnden Park for a number of years, and success on the field only returned in the 1950s with the signing of the legendary Nat Lofthouse.

'Lofty' was one of the great Boys' Own heroes of the age and his goals inspired Bolton to the FA Cup Final in 1953. That was the year of the 'Matthews Final' and indeed it was Stan's brilliance which finally broke plucky Wanderers. The 4–3 scoreline also created a new record for the competition, because never before had a side hit three goals in a final and lost!

In 1958, the Wanderers gained some consolation when they beat Manchester United 2–0 in a final which was emotionally affected following that tragic air crash in Munich which caused the death of so many of United's top players and officials.

During the early 1960s the Wanderers line-up went through a transitional period and results were anything but stable. The club eventually lost their place in the First Division in 1963/64 and though they were in the promotion hunt all the following season, they hit their worst spell in the run-in. In 1970/71 the Wanderers were relegated to the Third Division for the first time in their history.

They returned to Division Two as champions of the Third Division in 1972/73 and after five seasons of hard work returned to the top flight as Second Division champions. Frank Worthington topped the Division One scoring charts in 1978/79 but the following season was disastrous, as relegation was confirmed with five games remaining. The Wanderers were relegated to the Third Division in 1982/83 and four years later descended to the lowest division in the Football League.

Thankfully the Wanderers were promoted after just one season in Division Four, and in 1992/93 Bruce Rioch and Colin Todd led the club into the Endsleigh League Division One. During that season of 1993/94, the Wanderers reached the FA Cup sixth round but the following season made it all the way to Wembley, only to lose 2–1 to Liverpool in the Coca Cola Cup Final.

They returned to Wembley a few weeks later for the play-off final against Reading which the Wanderers won 4–3 after extra time. Relegated after just one season in the Premiership, Bolton won the First Division title at a canter, scoring 100 goals and securing 98 points. Sadly, despite moving to the Reebok Stadium, the Wanderers again failed to hold on to their Premiership status and were relegated after failing to get a result at Chelsea on the final day of the season.

Following the disappointments of 1997/98, the Wanderers fans had to endure the highs and lows of watching the club attempt to win back a place in the Premiership, and finally had to settle for a place in the play-offs against Ipswich Town. After a Michael Johansen goal had given Bolton a 1–0 lead to take to Portman Road no one could have imagined the emotional rollercoaster of a game in the second leg. Unfortunately, space prevents me from elaborating on a game that had everything. For the record the Wanderers lost 4–3 on the night but won through to the final at Wembley on the away goals rule. Sadly, they failed to take their chances against Graham Taylor's Watford side and went down 2–0. With the club facing another season of first division football the author, along with all other Bolton fans, hopes the Wanderers can make 1999/2000 a season to remember by gaining promotion to the top flight.

Dean Hayes
Bamber Bridge
May 1999

CHAPTER ONE

THE MANAGERS

Colin Todd.

Founder members of the Football League, Bolton Wanderers have had just nineteen managers since they made their first appointment in 1908. Yet in that total are five men who between them accumulated just over two and a half years service – Jimmy McIlroy, Jimmy Meadows, Charlie Wright, George Mulhall and Roy McFarland.

Bolton's first manager was John Somerville who had played in 293 games for the Trotters including the 1894 FA Cup Final against Notts County. He had been player-secretary and secretary-manager for ten years prior to his appointment as the club's first full-time manager. Under Somerville, the Wanderers had something of a yo-yo existence. They were promoted to the First Division in seasons 1899/1900, 1904/05 and 1908/09 but relegated in 1898/99, 1902/03 and 1907/08. When the club was relegated again in 1909/10 Somerville left the club and was replaced by Will Settle.

In his first full season in charge, he led the Wanderers to runners-up spot in the Second Division. The Trotters then finished fourth in Division One in 1911/12, sixth in 1913/14 and reached the FA Cup's semi-final the following season. Yet despite this relative success, some of Settle's responsibilities were taken away from him and he left the club under a cloud.

All the games Bolton played under Tom Mather were during the First World War when there were a number of occasions when the Wanderers' boss did not know whether he would be able to field a full side.

Bolton's fourth manager was Charles Foweraker who was to become the club's longest-serving and most successful manager. He was to put in twenty-five years' service (including four in wartime) during which Bolton won the FA Cup three times (a record he shares with John Nicholson of Sheffield United and Bill Nicholson of Tottenham Hotspur) and also came close to winning the League Championship on a number of occasions. Bolton did suffer some lean spells during Foweraker's time in charge but within two years of being relegated in 1932/33 he had steered them to promotion back to the First Division. When war was declared, he worked for the Wanderers on a voluntary basis but in August 1944 the popular Foweraker was forced to retire through ill-health.

After having played in 191 games for the Wanderers, Walter Rowley coached both the club's reserve and first team before replacing Charles Foweraker as manager. Though he led Bolton to victory in the League North Cup and to the semi-final of the FA Cup he too was forced to resign through ill-health after six years in charge, and was succeeded by Bill Ridding.

Ridding's term as Bolton manager stretched to nearly 18 years during which time he led the Wanderers to Wembley on two occasions. In 1953 the Trotters lost to Blackpool 4–3 after they had led 3–1 with just twenty minutes to go, but five years later they beat Manchester United 2–0, a result that was marred by the fact that most of the country wanted United to win because of the recent Munich air disaster. Towards the end of his tenure as Bolton manager, he had to fight to hold on to his better players and in August 1968 he left the Wanderers to run his own physiotherapy business.

Nat Lofthouse became temporary manager after the departure of Bill Ridding before the position became permanent after four months. When Jimmy McIlroy was appointed manager in November 1970 Lofthouse became general manager, but the Irishman was only in charge for 18 days, resigning after refusing to sell players directed by the board.

The Bolton board had a preference for selecting people who had served the club in some other capacity. Each of the first eight appointments up to and including Jimmy McIlroy in 1970 was, in effect, an internal promotion. When Jimmy Meadows replaced McIlroy in January 1971 he was the first stranger to Burnden Park. However, he was in charge for only 11 weeks and left with the club struggling at the bottom of the Second Division.

Jimmy Armfield, the former Blackpool and England full-back, was appointed Bolton manager immediately after the club had been relegated from the Second Division, and two seasons later led the club to the Third Division Championship. Attendances at Burnden Park quadrupled as the crowds were attracted back to watch the exciting football his teams played. Not surprisingly he received a number of offers from top-flight clubs and in October 1974 he left Burnden Park to take charge at Leeds United.

It was Armfield's assistant, Ian Greaves, who was appointed as the club's eleventh manager. After the Wanderers had finished their first season under Greaves' leadership in mid-table, he took them to a Football League Cup semi-final against Everton and in 1977/78 led them to the Second Division Championship. Sadly the club failed to establish itself in the top flight and Greaves was sacked in January 1980 with the Trotters at the bottom of the table.

His replacement was the Bolton coach, Stan Anderson, but at the end of the 1979/80 season the Wanderers were relegated. Despite funds being made available to strengthen the squad, Anderson had an unhappy time at Burnden Park and in May 1981 he was sacked. George Mulhall, who had returned to the club as Anderson's assistant, took charge and saved the Wanderers from relegation but after a row with the Bolton board over the sale of Paul Jones, he left to be replaced by John McGovern.

The former Nottingham Forest midfielder joined the club as player-manager in the summer of 1982 but at the end of his first season the club dropped into the Third Division. Results improved in 1983/84 following the introduction of a number of young players but he parted company with the club in January 1985 with the Wanderers near the foot of the Third Division.

Former Bolton 'keeper Charlie Wright was put in temporary charge and led the club to five consecutive victories. After he had been appointed on a permanent basis, the Wanderers went through a bad spell but recovered and avoided the drop into the League's basement. However, in December 1985 he left the club by mutual consent with Liverpool and England full-back Phil Neal becoming the Wanderers' player-manager.

In 1986 Neal led the club to the Freight Rover Trophy Final at Wembley where they lost 3–0 to Bristol City and though the Whites were relegated to the Fourth Division for the first time in their history, they won promotion at the first attempt. In 1989, Bolton returned to Wembley and beat Torquay United 4–1 in the Sherpa Van Trophy Final. Neal then took the club to the play-offs in 1990 and 1991 but the nearest they got to promotion was 1991 when they played Tranmere Rovers at Wembley and lost 1–0 after extra time. Neal left Burnden Park in May 1992 after six and a half years with the club.

Bruce Rioch, who had resigned as manager of Millwall only two months previously, took over the reins at Burnden Park. In his first season with the club he led them to promotion as runners-up in the Second Division. In 1993/94 Rioch's Wanderers won their way through to the sixth round of the FA Cup, beating Premier League sides Everton, Arsenal and Aston Villa after winning at Anfield in the previous season's competition. In 1994/95 the Wanderers reached the Football League Cup Final at Wembley, where they lost 2-1 to Liverpool and won promotion to the Premier League after beating Reading in a remarkable play-off final. Sadly, Rioch left the club in the summer of 1995 to take charge at Arsenal.

Bolton turned to Roy McFarland to manage the club for the first season in the Premiership with Colin Todd, who had also served under Rioch, remaining as his assistant. With only two wins before the turn of the year, it came as no surprise when the former Derby County and England defender was dismissed after just over six months in charge.

In January 1996 the Board promoted Todd to the manager's position, a move which many supporters felt should have happened immediately after Rioch's departure.

Though the results in the New Year improved, Todd failed to prevent the Trotters from relegation to the First Division. With money to spend following the sale of Curcic and Stubbs, Todd set about rebuilding the side and in 1996/97 the Wanderers won the First Division Championship, scoring 100 goals in the process and amassing a club record 98 points.

Bolton's second season of Premiership football was played at the new Reebok Stadium but despite Todd spending over £6 million to bolster the Wanderers' side, the club were relegated again when a point on the final day of the season at Chelsea would have seen them to safety.

Known as 'Johnny Surefoot' because of his reliable displays at right-back, John Somerville played in 293 League and Cup games for the Wanderers and appeared in the FA Cup Final of 1894 as well as helping the club win promotion in 1898/99. In 1898 he was appointed secretary-player when Frank Brettell left to join Tottenham Hotspur and had therefore been acting as secretary for ten years when he added managerial duties to his role. His first season in charge proved extremely successful as the Trotters collected their first championship trophy in winning the Second Division title after only a season's absence from the top flight. The following season saw a complete contrast when Somerville found that the players who had helped the club win promotion in 1908/09 were not good enough to keep the Wanderers in the First Division. In January 1910, with the club firmly entrenched at the foot of the First Division and beaten 4–1 in the FA Cup by Second Division Stockport County, the management of the club was handed over to Will Settle. Somerville had spent over £3,000 in transfer fees, all to no avail! He remained as secretary until the end of the season before going on to become a Football League linesman.

Will Settle's father, Miles Settle JP, joined the board of Bolton Wanderers in 1895, and in 1899 Will took his place, serving in the same capacity until January 1910 when he was appointed Bolton's manager in place of John Somerville. He was unable to prevent the Wanderers being relegated that season but in 1910/11, with the help of trainers George Eccles and Peter Bullough, he steered the Trotters to promotion at the first attempt. It was Settle who developed the great left-wing pairing of Joe Smith and Ted Vizard and brought many other fine players to Burnden Park including Alf Bentley, Jimmy Fay, Alex Donaldson, Bob Glendenning and Jimmy Seddon. On Christmas Eve 1912 he sold Tom Barber to Aston Villa, the profits paying for the roofing to the Great Lever Stand. In 1911/12 Wanderers finished fourth in the First Division, sixth in 1913/14 and in 1914/15, they reached the semi-finals of the FA Cup. Then wartime football replaced the League and Cup competitions and in 1915, after finding certain responsibilities had been taken away from him, he left the club under something of a cloud after 17 years' service.

Tom Mather was assistant secretary at Manchester City before joining the Wanderers in a similar capacity. Later he became secretary at Burnden Park and then secretary-manager in the summer of 1915. His record as manager of Bolton Wanderers is a difficult one to quantify because all the club's games under his charge were played during the First World War. The Chorley-born manager's term in office was one of the most difficult of any Bolton boss, for there were a number of occasions when he did not know whether he would be able to field a full side! He remained as manager in name only until July 1919 as he had been called up by the Royal Navy. Mather's assistant Charles Foweraker carried out his duties before taking over on a permanent basis.

After the hostilities, Mather became secretary-manager of Southend United before taking charge at Stoke. At the Victoria Ground he built a team to challenge at the highest level. After 12 years with the Potters he left to take over at Newcastle United but after little success left the club when war was declared. He returned to football in 1945 as manager of Leicester City, later ending his managerial career with Kilmarnock.

The most successful manager in the club's history, Charles Foweraker entered football in a part-time capacity in 1895, acting as a gateman and a checker when Burnden Park opened while also employed by the Lancashire and Yorkshire Railway Company. When Tom Mather was called up to join the Royal Navy in 1915, Foweraker stepped in and guided the Wanderers through the war years. In July 1919 he was appointed secretary-manager on a permanent basis at a salary of £400 per annum. He was in charge of the club throughout Bolton's most successful period during the 1920s when the Trotters won three FA Cup Finals at Wembley and were serious contenders for the First Division Championship. In July 1938 he was awarded the Football League's Long Service Medal in recognition of more than 21 years' service to the Wanderers. The Lancashire FA also presented him with a similar award and he served as vice-president of that organisation for many years. Foweraker strongly believed in the development of players under military age and from this belief rose the greatest of all the Wanderers' heroes, Nat Lofthouse. In August 1944 Charles Foweraker was forced to retire through ill-health, having completed 49 years' continuous service with the club. He died at his Bolton home in July 1950, aged 73.

Walter Rowley gave the Wanderers 38 years' service as player, coach and manager. The Little Hulton-born defender played his early football with local sides Farnworth Wednesday, Walkden Wednesday and Little Hulton Wednesday before joining Oldham Athletic in 1910. Two years later he signed for Bolton Wanderers, going on to play in 191 games for the Trotters after making his debut against West Bromwich Albion in February 1913. He was the Wanderers' twelfth man in their 1923 FA Cup Final success, missing the final after just finishing a suspension following his sending-off in the fifth round draw at Huddersfield Town. Injury forced his retirement in 1925 and he was appointed coach to the Wanderers' reserve team. He later became first team coach before being made manager in August 1944. At the end of his first season in charge the Wanderers beat Manchester United 3–2 on aggregate to take the League North Cup; in 1946 they reached the semi-finals of the FA Cup. The Trotters continued to make steady progress under Rowley but in October 1950 he was forced to resign owing to ill-health. He was awarded life membership of the club for services rendered before later returning to management, first with Middlesbrough and then Shrewsbury Town.

As a player, Bill Ridding had been a centre-forward playing for Tranmere Rovers and both Manchester clubs before a double cartilage injury forced his retirement at the age of 22. His association with the Wanderers began in 1946 when he was appointed trainer and after a temporary spell as manager following Rowley's resignation, he was officially appointed secretary-manager of the Wanderers in February 1951 when he also acted as the club's trainer. In 1953 he led the Wanderers to Wembley in the FA Cup Final only for them to lose 4–3 to Blackpool after they had led 3–1 with twenty minutes to play. Five years later he took the club to Wembley again with a team he had put together for £110 and this time had the pleasure of being on the winning side against Manchester United. The abolition of the maximum wage in 1961 proved disastrous for clubs like Bolton and Ridding had to fight to hold on to the Wanderers' better players. In August 1968 he left Burnden Park to concentrate on his physiotherapy practice, later joining Lancashire County Cricket Club in that capacity before dying at the age of 70 in September 1981.

Nat Lofthouse became temporary manager after Bill Ridding's departure and though the post was made permanent four months later, he had little money to spend on players and failed to find success. By his own admission, the club's favourite son wanted to move away from the team manager's role and become the club's general manager. He got his wish in November 1970 when Jimmy McIlroy took over team affairs but this arrangement was short-lived and Lofthouse was soon back in charge, albeit as caretaker manager. He stepped aside again in January 1971 as Jimmy Meadows took charge, his last act being to select the club's youngest-ever league side which defeated Sheffield United 2–1. Three months later he was back as manager after Meadows had left and faced the unenviable task of leading the club in their first ever relegation into the Third Division. When Jimmy Armfield was appointed in May 1971, Lofthouse became chief scout but in 1972, his 33 year association with the club ended. He returned in 1978 to become manager of the Executive Club but in 1985 he took charge as caretaker manager for the third time as Bolton beat Chesterfield 2–1. In October 1986 he capped a lifetime's service by becoming the club's president, a role he still fulfils with great pride and dignity.

A marvellously gifted inside-forward, Jimmy McIlroy won League Championship and FA Cup runners-up medals with Burnley where he made over 400 appearances. Winning 55 full caps for Northern Ireland, 34 in consecutive matches, he formed an amazing understanding with Danny Blanchflower. In March 1963 he joined Stoke City, helping the Potters win the Second Division Championship. When his playing days were over McIlroy became manager of Oldham Athletic, before returning to the Victoria Ground as Stoke's chief coach. On 4 November 1970 he was officially appointed team manager at Bolton. His first game in charge was a 1–0 defeat at Norwich City which was followed by a 2–0 reverse at Millwall. Unbelievably, on 22 November and after only 18 days in charge, the popular Irishman parted company with the club. He had refused to sell players as directed by the board because if they had left it would undoubtedly have weakened the team and it was obvious that he could not work within those constraints.

Jimmy Armfield, known as 'Gentleman Jim', won fame as Blackpool and England's full-back. One of Bloomfield Road's greatest-ever servants, he appeared in 627 games for the club before retiring in 1971. He gained the first of his 43 full caps for his country against Brazil in 1959 and won 37 of them in consecutive matches. He was appointed Bolton's manager on 19 May 1971 and immediately set about restoring the club's confidence. The colours reverted from the all-white to the traditional white shirts and navy-blue shorts and by the end of his first season in charge, he had transformed things so much that only 41 goals were conceded, the club's best defensive performance since 1925.

The foundations had been laid and in 1972/73 the benefits were reaped when the Trotters secured the Third Division Championship with 61 points. Clearly recognisable by his tracksuit and pipe, Armfield stood firm as the Wanderers blooded more youngsters alongside the shrewd signings of internationals Tony Dunne and Peter Thompson. In September 1974 Armfield finally gave way to an offer from Leeds United and took the Elland Road club to the 1975 European Cup Final, leaving three years later to become a full-time journalist.

Beginning his career with Manchester United, Ian Greaves won a League Championship medal in 1955/56 and in 1958 played in the FA Cup Final against the Wanderers. After making 75 appearances for United he joined Lincoln City before later ending his career with Oldham Athletic. His first managerial post was at Huddersfield Town and in 1970 he took the Terriers to the Second Division title, but after two seasons in the top flight the Yorkshire club suffered relegation in consecutive seasons to the Third Division. He left Leeds Road in 1974 after a boardroom struggle.

After two months of unemployment he joined the Wanderers as assistant manager to Jimmy Armfield and when he left for Leeds United, Greaves was appointed Wanderers' manager in October 1974.

At Bolton, Manager of the Month awards came his way in January 1975, November 1976, August 1977 and October 1977 and after taking the Wanderers to a League Cup semi-final in 1976/77 he was named as Second Division Manager of the Season as the club won that division's championship in 1977/78. He broke the club transfer record four times before his dismissal in January 1980, with Bolton firmly rooted at the foot of the First Division. There were many who likened his departure to a 'death in the family'.

Stan Anderson captained Sunderland, Newcastle and Middlesbrough and was capped twice by England. A tough-tackling wing-half, he played in 402 league games for the Wearsiders and also appeared in two FA Cup semi-finals. He joined Newcastle United in November 1963 and played an important part in their Second Division championship-winning season of 1964/65. After joining Middlesbrough, first as player-coach, he was appointed manager in April 1966 and brought about a revival at Ayresome Park, leading the club back to the Second Division in 1966/67. After twice going close to promotion to the First Division, he left to manage AEK Athens.

He joined the Wanderers as coach under manager Ian Greaves. When Greaves was dismissed in January 1980 Anderson took over as caretaker manager before the appointment was made official the following month. At the end of that season, though, the Wanderers were relegated. Despite being given the money to strengthen the squad, the results didn't improve and in March 1981 George Mulhall returned to Burnden Park as Anderson's assistant. It was his return that coincided with the club's run to safety, and in May 1981 Stan Anderson was sacked with two years of his contract still to run.

Joining Aberdeen in 1953, George Mulhall scored 42 goals in 150 games for the Pittodrie club and won a Scottish League Cup Winners' medal in 1959 before leaving to join Sunderland in 1962. At Roker Park he scored 66 goals in 284 appearances, helping the club to promotion to Division One in 1963/64.

In October 1971 the Scottish international winger joined Halifax Town as trainer-coach before being appointed manager eight months later. He arrived at Burnden Park in October 1974 as assistant to Ian Greaves before leaving to become manager at Bradford City in 1978. He returned to Bolton for a second spell with the club in March 1981 and was appointed manager in June of that year. Despite a number of problems – six players released, six players placed on the transfer list and the chief coach and scout leaving – Mulhall saved the Trotters from relegation. However, there was conflict between Mulhall and the board over the sale of Paul Jones and in June 1982 he left the club. Mulhall later worked as assistant to Frank Worthington at Tranmere before working as chief scout, youth development officer and assistant manager at Huddersfield Town. He is now manager of Halifax Town.

As a player, John McGovern followed Brian Clough around from club to club and captained Nottingham Forest to two European Cup Final successes. He had made his Football League debut as a 16-year-old for Hartlepool United and, after helping Derby County into the First Division in 1969, he was the youngest player to have appeared in all four divisions. In all, he made 545 league appearances for Hartlepool United, Derby County, Leeds United and Nottingham Forest.

He joined Bolton Wanderers as player-manager in June 1982 and had little success and a lot of bad luck during his time in charge. At the end of his first season the Trotters lost their Second Division status and with no money available to strengthen the squad, McGovern took a drop in wages, ran in a fund-raising marathon and organised supporters' evenings. During 1983/84 an influx of younger players such as Warren Joyce, Neil Redfern and Steve Thompson brought some good results and positive play but the following season with the Wanderers sixth from bottom of the Third Division, he parted company with the club. Sadly for the Bolton fans he had made just 16 league appearances in two and a half years as player-manager.

After winning a Third Division championship medal with the Wanderers in 1972/73, Charlie Wright was forced to retire with a back injury. He remained at Burnden Park as youth team coach before moving to York City where he was manager for three years. In August 1981 he returned to Bolton, initially as reserve team coach before, following John McGovern's departure in January 1985, he was put in temporary charge. Within three weeks he had led the Whites to five consecutive victories, the club's best winning sequence in six years, and on 7 February 1985 he was named as Bolton's manager. Incredibly the Wanderers only won one of their next 10 games but because of a good run in April, avoided relegation. Although he signed some useful and experienced players, he left the club by mutual consent in December 1985, ending his Bolton career in exactly the opposite way to which it had started with five consecutive defeats!

Beginning his league career with Northampton Town, Phil Neal made 206 first team appearances for the Cobblers before joining Liverpool for £65,000 in October 1974. He made his debut for the Reds against Everton the following month as a replacement for the injured Alec Lindsey at left-back. From his second appearance for the club in December 1974 until injury caused him to miss Liverpool's game with Sunderland in October 1983, Phil Neal played in 366 consecutive league games. Neal was an intelligent positional player who denied the winger any space. Excellent in defence, his distribution was immaculate. The most capped England right-back with 50 caps to his name, he won almost every honour while playing for Liverpool. He won seven League Championship medals and was on the winning side in four League Cup Finals. He won a UEFA Cup Winners' medal and four European Cup Winners' medals – only an FA Cup Winners' medal eluded him.

Halfway through the 1985/86 season, he left Anfield to join Bolton as player-manager. He continued to play until 1988/89 lending his experience to the younger players. His first few years in management were quite eventful. In 1986 he led the side to Wembley where they lost 3–0 to Bristol City in the Freight Rover Trophy Final. In 1986/87 the club were relegated to the Fourth Division for the first time in their history but bounced back at the end of the following campaign. There was another visit to Wembley in 1989 when the Wanderers beat Torquay United 4–1 to win the Sherpa Van Trophy. Neal left the club at the end of the 1991/92 season. He had helped bring stability to the Wanderers along with a measure of success but the pressure of poor results and declining attendances prompted the bombshell. After a period of involvement with the England management team Neal took charge of both Coventry City and Cardiff City.

Scottish international wing-half Bruce Rioch played for
Luton Town, Aston Villa, Derby County, Everton,
Birmingham City, Sheffield United and Torquay United,
where he gained his first experience of management.
However, his first success came following his appointment
by Middlesbrough in February 1986. He guided the club
from a dire financial position and lifted them from the
Third to the First Division within two seasons. Rioch left
Ayresome Park in March 1990 and in less than a month was
in charge at Millwall.

In 1990/91 he took the London club to the Second
Division play-offs but after their form slumped he left to
join the Wanderers in March 1992. He achieved promotion
in his first season at Burnden Park as the Wanderers finished
runners-up in Division Two. That season the Wanderers
beat Liverpool at Anfield before losing to Derby County in
the fifth round. In 1993/94 he led Bolton to the sixth
round of the FA Cup before taking the club to the League
Cup Final and promotion to the Premiership via the play-
offs the following season. In June 1995 Rioch left the
Wanderers to manage Arsenal but after 15 months he was
sacked and joined Queen's Park Rangers. He is now
manager of Norwich City.

Signed from Tranmere Rovers, Roy McFarland
formed an excellent partnership with Dave Mackay,
helping Derby County win the Second Division
championship in 1968/9. After winning the first of
28 caps for England he became an inspirational captain
as Derby won their first league title in 1972. He went
on to appear in 530 games for the Rams, scoring 48
goals. In his first managerial role he took Bradford
City to Division Three in 1982 but was then enticed
to rejoin Derby as assistant manager. He took over as
caretaker when Peter Taylor was sacked and remained
at the Baseball Ground as Arthur Cox's assistant until
October 1993 when he became manager. But after
26 years' service with the club he left to take charge at
Bolton in June 1995, with his former Derby County
team-mate Colin Todd remaining in the assistant's
post. The Wanderers' first season in the Premier
League was always likely to be a hard time for the
club, and with just two wins before the turn of the
year Bolton were on course for a swift return to the
First Division. The poor run of results culminated in
Bolton dismissing McFarland. After a short spell out
of the game he returned to take charge at
Cambridge United.

Colin Todd was an elegant and poised player who was always comfortable on the ball. He developed a great partnership with Roy McFarland at Derby which was later transferred into the England team. Todd won two League Championship medals with the Rams and in 1974/75 was voted the PFA's Footballer of the Year. He later helped Birmingham win promotion to the First Division and Oxford United the Third Division championship. After managing Whitley Bay he became assistant manager to Bruce Rioch at Middlesbrough, eventually succeeding him as manager. In May 1991 he resigned and a year later became Rioch's assistant again, this time at Bolton Wanderers. He played an important role in the club's promotion to the Premier League and in the Wanderers' cup exploits which culminated in their reaching the League Cup Final at Wembley in 1995. When Rioch left for Arsenal, Todd remained as assistant to newly appointed manager Roy McFarland, but when he was dismissed in January 1996 Todd became manager.

Though there was an improvement in the club's fortunes in the second half of the campaign, Todd couldn't prevent the club from being relegated. Todd then sold Sasa Curcic to Aston Villa and Alan Stubbs to Celtic for a combined fee of £7.5 million and bought Danes Per Frandsen and Michael Johansen for around £2.5 million. The 1996/97 season saw the Wanderers run away with the First Division championship. Sixteen wins from 19 games secured promotion by 5 April with five games still to play and the championship was taken in grand style at Maine Road four days later. All that remained was for Bolton to score a century of goals and amass a ton of points. Two goals at Tranmere Rovers on the last day sorted out the first part of the equation but a last-minute equaliser left Bolton stranded on 98 points. In the 1997 close season Todd bought Neil Cox and Robbie Elliott and, as the season got under way, Peter Beardsley and Mark Fish. He then paid a club record fee of £3.5 million for Wimbledon's Dean Holdsworth but the Wanderers were still relegated after failing to get a result at Stamford Bridge on the final day of the season.

CHAPTER TWO

1888–1914

Bolton Wanderers, 1893.

Bolton Wanderers played their first game in the Football League on 8 September 1888 when they entertained Derby County at Pikes Lane. The club's first international player, Kenny Davenport, had the distinction of scoring Bolton's first league goal after only two minutes' play. He scored again a minute later and with James Brogan netting soon after, the Wanderers were 3–0 up with just five minutes played. Unfortunately Derby came back to lead at half-time and won the game 6–3.

In 1889-90 the Wanderers finished fourth from bottom of the League and had to apply for re-election. Aston Villa had finished ahead of Bolton on goal average, the difference being one-hundredth of a goal! However, the Wanderers claimed that their home defeat by Notts County had been 3–0 and not 4–0 therefore placing the club above Villa. The League ruling was that both Villa and Bolton should stay in the competition without having to apply for re-election, this being the closest that the club have ever come to losing their Football League status. That season the Wanderers recorded their biggest victory in first-class football with a 13–0 win over Sheffield United in the FA Cup second round, with Jimmy Cassidy scoring five of the goals.

The club reached their first-ever FA Cup Final in 1894 but lost 4–1 to Second Divison Notts County at Goodison Park.

In 1895 the Wanderers left Pikes Lane and moved to Burnden Park, winning their first league game against Everton on 14 September by 3–1. They ended the season in fourth place in Division One and lost to Sheffield Wednesday in the semi-finals of the FA Cup after a replay.

However, it wasn't too long before the club encountered its first real crisis, for after a good start to the 1896/97 season the team went into decline, winning only two of its last ten matches. The Wanderers were badly in need of a manager to take charge of team affairs; instead it was left to a number of the club's directors who couldn't agree over team selection. Players became dissatisfied and one, Jim McGeachan, was suspended when he refused to accompany the team to a match in Sheffield. Because of a lack of money available for players' wages seven first-teamers left the club, and in 1898/99 the club suffered their first-ever relegation despite four wins in the last eight games of the the season.

The Wanderers won promotion at the first attempt as runners-up to Sheffield Wednesday, who were the Wanderers' opponents on 18 January 1902 when goalkeeper John Sutcliffe became the first Bolton player to be sent off at Burnden Park in the club's 3–1 win.

The 1902/03 season saw the Wanderers make their worst-ever start to a Football League season when they lost their first seven games. However, the next 15 games resulted in three draws and 12 defeats before a 3–1 win at Notts County in the club's twenty-third game of the campaign! Despite eight victories in the last 12 games of the season, the Wanderers finished bottom of the League and were relegated.

The following season Bolton went all-out to win promotion but just failed at the final hurdle. However, they did win through to the FA Cup Final against Championship-chasing Manchester City and though they outplayed their First Division opponents for much of the game, they were beaten 1–0 thanks to a disputed goal from Welsh international Billy Meredith.

In 1904/05 the Wanderers finished the season as runners-up to Liverpool in the Second Division and on their return to the top flight were the league's top scorers with 81 goals, with Sam Marsh and Walter White netting 50 of them. After two successful seasons the Wanderers were relegated for a third time in 1907/08. The Second Division Championship came to Burnden Park for the first time the following season but in 1909/10 the club lost their First Division status after just one season. Bolton were known as the 'yo-yo' club, for in 1910/11 they won promotion at the first time of asking, a campaign which also saw the forming of the left-wing partnership of Joe Smith and Ted Vizard.

In 1914/15, the last season of League football before the First World War, the Wanderers recorded their best away win with a 7–1 defeat of Aston Villa and reached the semi-finals of the FA Cup where they lost to the eventual winners, Sheffield United.

JAMES BROGAN

One of the Wanderers' first professional players, James Brogan was a Scotsman of Irish descent who played for the club before the formation of the Football League. After playing for Beith and Edinburgh Hibernian, Brogan signed for Heart of Midlothian and it was while they were on a tour of Lancashire that the forward impressed the Wanderers. He signed for the club in December 1884 and over the years proved himself a useful goalscorer whether he played at inside or outside-left. In December 1888 he netted five of Bolton's goals as Sunderland were beaten 10–1, and it was this kind of form that led to his selection for Lancashire.

He scored one of the goals in the club's inaugural Football League match when they lost 6–3 to Derby County and ended the season in which he was ever-present as the club's leading marksman with 13 goals. The following season he hit a hat-trick in the 13–0 defeat of Sheffield United in a second round FA Cup match. Losing his place to James Turner midway through the 1891/92 season, Brogan left the club and went to work in the shipyards where he remained until he was 85 years old!

Welsh international full-back Di Jones, as he was more popularly known, played his early football with his home-town team of Oswestry before moving to Chirk and captaining them to victory in the Welsh Cup of 1885. After a short spell with Newton Heath he joined Bolton in 1888, and played in 12 games during the inaugural season of the Football League. Over the next ten seasons, Jones missed very few games for the Wanderers and was ever-present in seasons 1891/92 and 1892/93 when the club finished fifth in the First Division. He had been appointed as the Wanderers' captain in 1890 and led the side that reached the 1894 FA Cup Final where they lost 4–1 to Notts County. He was awarded a benefit match against Preston North End in September 1895 in what was the first football game to be played at Burnden Park, but in October 1898 after playing in 255 League and Cup games he left the Wanderers to join Manchester City. He led the Ardwick club to the Second Division title but in August 1902 he gashed his knee in a practice game, contracted tetanus and died a few days later.

Though he was born in Staffordshire, James Turner was brought up in Lancashire and joined the Wanderers along with his brother Richard in 1888. Playing at outside-left he scored on his debut as Bolton beat Notts County 7–3 in March 1889. Over the next couple of seasons his appearances were limited, and it wasn't until the 1891/92 season when he moved to wing-half that he began to establish himself as a first team regular. His performances led to him winning a full cap for England in a 6–0 win against Wales at Stoke in March 1893. That month also saw him involved in an incident in a Lancashire Cup tie at Bury. As he tangled with an opponent the home crowd rushed on to attack him, leaving the referee with no alternative but to abandon the game! Turner, who scored 12 goals in 108 League and Cup games, left Bolton in September 1894 to join Stoke. He later played for Derby County where he appeared in their FA Cup Final defeat against Nottingham Forest before returning to the Victoria Ground to end his career.

Kilmarnock-born centre-forward James Cassidy began his career with his home-town club before playing for Glasgow Hibernian, from whom the Wanderers signed him in 1889. His first league appearance for the club came in a 6–3 defeat at West Bromwich Albion while in only his fifth game for the Wanderers he scored four goals in a 7–1 win over Derby County. He ended that season as the club's leading scorer with 20 goals in 19 League and Cup games – a feat he was to achieve on five occasions. Included in this total were five goals in the club's record 13–0 FA Cup win over Sheffield United.

When Bolton beat Notts County 2-0 in March 1892, Cassidy became the first Wanderers player to score from the penalty spot. He also scored one of Bolton's goals in the 3–1 win over Everton in what was the first league game played at Burnden Park. He had scored 101 goals in 219 games when he left Bolton to play for Newton Heath. After a couple of seasons he joined neighbours Manchester City before later ending his career with Middlesbrough.

Born at Shibden, near Halifax, John Sutcliffe won international honours at both rugby and soccer. He played rugby union for both Bradford and Heckmondwike and while with the latter won an England cap against New Zealand in 1889. Towards the end of that year the Yorkshire club were suspended for professionalism and so Sutcliffe decided to try his hand at soccer and joined the Wanderers. He arrived at the club as a forward, but after his rugby instincts became apparent he switched to goalkeeper and made his debut in a 7–0 home win over West Bromwich Albion at Pikes Lane in December 1889. The following season he became the club's regular custodian, a position he held for the next 11 seasons. Sutcliffe, who played for the Football League on three occasions, won the first of five caps for England in March 1893 when he played against Wales at Stoke.

However, he also had the unenviable distinction of being the first Bolton player to receive his marching orders at Burnden Park when he was sent off for dissent in a 3–1 win over Sheffield Wednesday. Sutcliffe went on to appear in 364 games for the Wanderers before leaving to join Millwall in the summer of 1902. He later had spells with Manchester United and Plymouth Argyle, then in the Southern League, before becoming coach at Southend United. After the First World War he was appointed trainer at Bradford City.

After appearing at centre-forward for Vale of Leven in the 1890 Scottish Cup Final, Alec Paton signed for West Manchester from whom he joined the Wanderers later that year. He made his debut in the opening game of the 1890/91 season in a 4–2 home win over Notts County. Having been converted to half-back he was ever-present in his first three seasons with the club, and didn't miss a game until Boxing Day 1893 after 98 consecutive League and Cup games following his debut.

Paton was a fearless player; in 1894 he played in the FA Cup Final against Notts County covered in bandages! He recovered to become a regular in the half-back line again, missing just one game in the next three seasons. At the end of the 1897/98 season he refused to re-sign after a disagreement over pay, and although the differences were resolved he only played in a further five league games as the club lost their First Division status for the first time. Having had the distinction of appearing in both the Scottish and English Cup Finals, Paton ended his Bolton career with 15 goals in 241 League and Cup games.

Glasgow-born Archie Freebairn played his early football with Wheatburn and Partick Thistle before joining the Wanderers in 1894. He made his debut in the opening game of the 1894/95 season in a 2–2 draw at home to Stoke. A strong-tackling half-back, Freebairn was a model of consistency, for in five seasons between 1894/95 and 1898/99 he missed just two games. His 136 consecutive league appearances in that spell is a club record.

During the 1898/99 season Freebairn was appointed as the Wanderers' captain in place of Di Jones but despite one or two encouraging results, he couldn't prevent the club being relegated for the first time in their history. In 1899/1900 he played his part in helping the club win promotion at the first attempt. He continued to be a first team regular and appeared in the Bolton side that lost 1–0 to Manchester City in the FA Cup Final of 1904. He played the last of his 315 League and Cup games for the Wanderers in a 3–2 home defeat by Birmingham in March 1907, and though he stayed a further three years they were spent playing reserve team football.

Bob Brown began his Football League career with Sheffield Wednesday and scored two goals for the Owls in a 5–2 win over Accrington in the club's opening fixture at Olive Grove. A versatile player, he appeared in seven different positions for the Yorkshire club in 1894/95 before joining Third Lanark for a short spell. He joined the Wanderers in the summer of 1895 and played against Everton in the first league game to be played at Burnden Park. That season he helped the club finish fourth in Division One but the majority of the 1896/97 campaign was spent on loan at Burnley. He returned to Bolton for the following season and played in the sides that suffered relegation in 1898/99 and won promotion in 1899/1900. Brown, who in the latter stages of his career played in every position except goalkeeper and full-back, made 136 League and Cup appearances for the Wanderers.

Bob Jack began his football career with his home-town club Alloa Athletic before joining Bolton in 1895. The tricky winger made his debut for the Wanderers in a 2–1 win at Small Heath in September 1895, and after that was a regular member of the club's first team for five seasons. In 1896/97 the winger was the club's top scorer with 11 goals in 28 League games, while in 1899/1900 he helped the Wanderers win promotion to the First Division. Jack went on to score 29 goals in 125 League and Cup games before leaving to join Preston North End. After just one season at Deepdale in which the Lilywhites narrowly missed out on promotion to the top flight, he signed for Glossop.

In 1903 he moved into the Southern League with Plymouth Argyle, later becoming their manager, a position he later held at Southend. He returned to Home Park as secretary-manager before leaving to join Clapton in 1929. Bob Jack's three sons, David, Rollo and Donald, all appeared for the Wanderers.

Jocky Wright joined Bolton from Clyde in the summer of 1895 and made his debut at inside-left in a 2–0 defeat at Stoke on the opening day of the 1895/96 season. Along with Alec Paton, Wright was ever-present as the Wanderers ended the season in fourth place in Division One. Though not a prolific scorer, he netted one of the goals in the Wanderers' 2–0 win over Bury in February 1896 in what was the first FA Cup tie to be played at Burnden Park. He had scored 17 goals in 94 games for the Wanderers when in October 1898 Sheffield Wednesday paid £200 for his services. In 1899/1900 Wright was the Yorkshire club's leading scorer with 26 goals as along with the Wanderers they were promoted to the First Division. After 110 games for the Owls he returned to Bolton for a second spell in March 1902, taking his tally of goals to 22 in 128 appearances.

Laurie Bell first made his name as a centre-forward with Dumbarton before leaving to play with Third Lanark. In 1897 he joined Sheffield Wednesday but, unable to break into the first team, moved to Everton where his brother Jack played. Looking to strengthen their squad following relegation to the Second Division in 1898/99, the Wanderers remembered Bell's performances against them and recruited his services in the summer of 1899. The Scotsman scored the club's first-ever goal in the Second Division after 12 minutes of the game at Loughborough Town which Bolton won 3–2. The Wanderers were promoted at the end of the season and Bell was top scorer with 23 goals, including a hat-trick in the return fixture with Loughborough which Bolton won 7–0, and four goals in the final game of the season when Burton Swifts were beaten 5–0. After breaking his leg against Newton Heath in April 1902 he recovered to take his total of goals for Bolton to 45 in 103 games before leaving to join Brentford.

David Stokes was playing for Brierley Hill Alliance when he joined Aston Villa on Birmingham and District League forms. Though he was on Villa's books he continued to turn out for Brierley Hill and in December 1901 Bolton secured his services. Villa reported the Burnden Park club to the League and they were fined 10 guineas, while they had to give Stokes a free transfer. After making his Wanderers' debut in a 2–1 win at Wolves, Stokes scored the first of 46 goals for Bolton in a 2–2 draw against Villa! Over the next 15 seasons Stokes missed very few games and was ever-present in 1905/06 and 1907/08. He won a Second Division Championship medal in 1908/09 and represented the Football League on a number of occasions.

He continued to play for the Wanderers after the First World War but in September 1920, after taking his total of first team appearances to 420, he left and returned to play for Brierley Hill Alliance. The following year Wolves brought him out of non-league obscurity, and he made seven appearances in their league side of 1920/21.

Left-back Bob Struthers began his career with Everton but having failed to make much of an impression left to play non-league football with Gravesend United. He then joined Portsmouth and it was from the Fratton Park club that Bolton signed him in the summer of 1901. He made his debut in a 2–0 defeat at Small Heath on the opening day of the 1901/02 season but only played in two other games that campaign. Midway through the following season he won a regular place in the Bolton side and after appearing in the 1904 FA Cup Final helped the Wanderers win promotion to the First Division in 1904/05. He went on to play in 141 League and Cup games before leaving Bolton in August 1907 to play for Bradford. At the end of his only season with the Yorkshire club they won election to the Second Division of the Football League.

Sam Greenhalgh joined the Wanderers in the summer of 1902 after playing his early football with local sides Eagley and Turton. He made his debut in a 2–0 home defeat by Sheffield Wednesday on the opening day of the 1902/03 season. That campaign saw Greenhalgh make 30 appearances but at the end of it the Wanderers were relegated. The club's regular centre-half, he appeared in the 1904 FA Cup Final when Bolton lost 1–0 to Manchester City and in 1904/05 helped the Wanderers win promotion from the Second Division.

Greenhalgh, who had represented the Football League, left Burnden Park in October 1905 to join Aston Villa but within two years had returned and in 1909 was an important member of the Bolton side that won the Second Division Championship. After just one season in the top flight the club were relegated, but Greenhalgh, who by now had been appointed club captain, led them to promotion in 1911/12. Towards the end of his Bolton career Greenhalgh, who scored 20 goals in 278 games, was given a six-week suspension by the club after refusing to play on the wing in an emergency. He later left the club to end his career with Chorley.

Goalscoring forward Sam Marsh played his early football with Daisy Hill and Atherton Church House before joining the Wanderers in 1902. Though the club were relegated at the end of his first season at Burnden Park, Marsh scored nine goals in a ten-game spell towards the end of the campaign and was the club's top scorer.

In 1903/04 Marsh netted 21 League and Cup goals including hat-tricks against Gainsborough Trinity (Home 5–0) and Barnsley (Home 5–1). The following season he formed a prolific goalscoring partnership with Albert Shepherd and Walter White and scored 27 goals including a hat-trick against Burton United (Home 7–1) to top the scoring charts for a third successive season. Though he was to remain at Burnden until 1912, his appearances for the Wanderers' first team were restricted because of the arrival of John Owen. After captaining the reserves to success in the Manchester Cup in 1909 he returned to the first team at wing-half, but after scoring 81 goals in 201 games and helping the club win promotion to the First Division, he left to play for Bury.

Scottish international forward Walter White missed very few games in six seasons with the Wanderers after joining them from Hurlford Thistle in the summer of 1902. After playing in the 1904 FA Cup Final defeat against Manchester City, he scored 24 goals in 33 league games in 1904/05 as the Wanderers won promotion to the First Division. Included in this total were hat-tricks against Burton United (Home 7-1) and Doncaster Rovers (Away 4-0). His goalscoring continued in the top flight as he netted 25 goals in 38 games including a spell of 7 goals in 5 games. He had scored 93 goals in 217 games when following the club's relegation in 1907/08 he left to join Everton.

He helped the Goodison club to runners-up in the League in 1908/09, his first season, and to the FA Cup semi-finals the following season. He left soon afterwards to join Fulham where he ended his career having played in 193 games for the Cottagers.

Scottish winger Marshall McEwan began his career with Blackpool and had made 45 appearances for the Bloomfield Road club when Bolton signed him in February 1905. His only appearance for the Wanderers in that promotion-winning season of 1904/05 came in a home match against Bradford City which Bolton won 2–0. However, after just one game of the following season, McEwan found himself in favour and over the next five campaigns missed very few matches. Though not a prolific scorer, netting just 15 goals in 164 games, his wing-play created many goalscoring opportunities for the likes of Albert Shepherd and Walter White.

After helping the club win promotion in 1908/09, McEwan joined Chelsea midway through the following season as the Wanderers' finances necessitated such a sale. On leaving Stamford Bridge McEwan played for Linfield before ending his career with non-league Fleetwood.

Bolton-born centre-forward Albert Shepherd made his debut for his home-town club in a 5–1 home win over Gainsborough Trinity on 5 November 1904 and went on to score 15 goals in 24 League games as the Wanderers won promotion to the First Division.

In 1905/06 Shepherd was the club's top scorer with 26 goals in 31 games including four against Nottingham Forest (Home 6–0) and Sunderland (Home 6–2). That form earned him international recognition and in April 1906 he scored England's goal in a 2–1 defeat by Scotland. He was the club's leading scorer again in 1906/07 with 19 goals including a hat-trick in a 6–1 home win over Sheffield United. Though the Wanderers were relegated in 1907/08 Shepherd continued to find the net, scoring 25 goals in 29 league games including hat-tricks against Bury (Home 3–6); Woolwich Arsenal (Home 3–1) and Newcastle United (Home 4–0). The Magpies were the club that Shepherd joined after the Wanderers had made a poor start to the 1908/09 season. He had scored 90 goals in 123 games for Bolton and continued his prolific scoring for Newcastle, topping their charts for the next three seasons and scoring both goals in their 1910 FA Cup Final victory over Barnsley.

Signed from Brierley Hill Alliance in the summer of 1905, Herbert Baverstock played in 79 consecutive League games immediately following his debut in a 3–3 draw at Notts County on 9 September 1905. Baverstock was the club's first-choice right-back until November 1921. When the Wanderers won the Second Division Championship in 1908/09, Baverstock played in all but one game and scored his first goal for the club in a 4–0 home win over Gainsborough Trinity. Though the Wanderers were relegated after just one season in the top flight, Baverstock showed his versatility in 1910/11, when the club once again won promotion, by playing the majority of the season at left-back. He was still in the Wanderers' side after the First World War and had made 388 appearances before losing his first team place to Bob Haworth.

The Bolton Wanderers side were on tour in Scotland in 1893. Secretary J.J. Bentley signed the card, wishing the recipient a Happy New Year.

Goalkeeper John Edmondson began his career with his home-town club Accrington Stanley before joining Manchester City in the summer of 1902. Though his first team opportunities at Hyde Road were limited owing to the fine form of Jack Hillman, Edmondson was one of a number of players suspended in an illegal payments scandal at the club. The ban was eventually lifted and in December 1906 Bolton paid £600 to bring Edmondson to Burnden Park. He made his debut in a 3–0 home win over Liverpool on New Year's Day 1907 and went on to be the club's first-choice custodian for the next nine seasons. He was ever-present in Bolton's Second Division Championship-winning season of 1908/09 and appeared in 259 first team games before his retirement in 1915.

Tom Barber joined the Wanderers in May 1908 from north-east side West Stanley and made his debut in a goalless draw at home to Fulham. Able to play in a variety of positions, he scored two goals in his first game at centre-forward as Bolton beat Burnley 3–1 at Turf Moor in March 1911. In 1911/12 Barber was the club's only ever-present as they finished fourth in Division One. He went on to score 14 goals in 107 League and Cup games before being transferred to Aston Villa for a fee of £1,950 on Christmas Eve 1912. The profits from Barber's transfer allowed the Wanderers to cover the Great Lever Stand. Barber's greatest moment in a Villa shirt was when he scored the only goal in the 1913 FA Cup Final against Sunderland. After leaving Villa Park he had spells with Stalybridge and Merthyr before joining Walsall in 1921. Sadly, he died from tuberculosis just four years later.

Signed from Tranmere Rovers, Harold Hilton joined Bolton in March 1910 and played in the last four games of the 1909/10 season which saw the Wanderers relegated to the Second Division. The following season he scored 13 goals in 30 games to help the club win promotion at the first attempt, seven of his strikes coming in the last eight games of the season. In December 1911 Hilton was injured in the Wanderers' 3–2 defeat at Notts County and was out of the game for 15 months. However, when he did attempt a comeback he was injured in his first game and did not play again until November 1914. This time he scored the opening goal of the game after just a matter of seconds as Bolton went on to beat Spurs 4–2. He stayed with Bolton until after the First World War but in May 1921, after scoring 24 goals in 65 games, he returned to Tranmere Rovers on a free transfer.

Full-back Jack Feebury joined the Wanderers from Hucknall in 1908, though it was September 1909 before he made his first team debut in a 3–0 home win over Woolwich Arsenal. He soon became an established member of the Wanderers' side and was noted for his powerful shooting. In 1910/11 he helped the Wanderers win promotion to the First Division, his only goal of the season being a spectacular long-range effort which secured a point in a 2–2 draw at Derby County. Having already won a Players' Union kicking contest in August 1913, Feebury, who scored 16 goals in 192 games for Bolton, scored four goals in four successive games in the 1919/20 season, although two of these were from the penalty spot. At the end of that season Feebury left the Wanderers and joined Exeter City. He later played for Brighton before ending his playing days with Mid-Rhondda.

Alex Donaldson was playing non-league football for Ripley Athletic when the Wanderers signed him for a fee of just £50 in December 1911. He had to wait until the beginning of the following season before making his first team debut in a 1–0 home win over Chelsea. His form in the seasons leading up to the First World War was such that it earned him international recognition when he played for Scotland against Wales at Glasgow in 1914.

He returned to Burnden Park after the hostilities and was the club's first-choice outside-right until he fractured his right kneecap in a 2-1 win at Preston North End in February 1921. When he did regain full fitness he found his position occupied by Billy Butler, and he left Bolton to play for Sunderland after scoring six goals in 146 games. After a season at Roker Park he returned to the north-west to play for Manchester City, later ending his career with non-league Chorley.

Southport-born Jimmy Fay played his early football with a number of local sides before turning professional in 1903 and joining Chorley and later Oswaldtwistle Rovers. After signing for Oldham Athletic he made his first appearance at Hudson Fold in the 1905/06 season against Atherton Church in the Lancashire Combination 'A' Division. Between 1907/08 and 1910/11 he did not miss a league game for Oldham and was the club's leading scorer in 1909/10 with 26 goals from inside-forward. A hat-trick against Barnsley led to a local tailor's shop giving the Oldham player an overcoat to mark his achievement!

After a disagreement about his continuing to live in Southport, he left the Latics and joined the Wanderers. He made his name with Bolton as a centre-half but was laid up for most of 1913 with a hernia. He played for the Wanderers on both sides of the First World War and in April 1919 represented the Football League against the Scottish League. He played in 136 games for Bolton before returning to play at Southport Central where he had played at the outbreak of war. Fay was secretary of the PFA from 1922 to 1952 (and chairman 1922–9), having been a founder member of the old Players' Union in 1907.

A former Welsh schoolboy international, Billy Jennings joined Bolton in the summer of 1912 and made his debut for the Wanderers in a 1–1 draw at home to Derby County in November of that year. Just as he seemed to have established himself in the Bolton side he was injured in the Boxing Day clash against Sheffield United and forced to miss the rest of the season. When Jennings won the first of his 11 caps for Wales in 1914 he was still in the Wanderers' Central League side, but when League football resumed after the First World War he won a regular place at half-back. When Bolton won the FA Cup in 1923 Jennings played in all seven FA Cup ties and was a member of the side when Wanderers beat Manchester City 1–0 in 1926, to take the Cup for a second time. He played in 287 League and Cup games for the Wanderers before hanging up his boots in 1931. After two years out of the game he became coach at Notts County, a post he later held at Cardiff City before being appointed manager of the Ninian Park club.

A magnificent centre-forward and inspirational captain, Joe Smith began his career as an amateur with Newcastle St Luke's in the Staffordshire League before joining the Wanderers. He made his league debut in a 2–0 defeat at West Bromwich Albion in April 1909 before establishing himself as a first team regular in 1910/11. His performances for the Wanderers in the years up to the First World War led to him winning the first of five full caps for England in February 1913 in a 2–1 defeat against Ireland. Smith played in 51 wartime games for the Wanderers, scoring 48 goals, including six against Stoke in September 1916 as Bolton won 9–2. He 'guested' for Chelsea along with Ted Vizard while serving in the RAF and in 1918 they both helped the Stamford Bridge club win the London v. Lancashire Cup Final.

He was Bolton's most consistent scorer until Nat Lofthouse, and his 38 goals which included hat-tricks against Middlesbrough (Home 6-2) Sunderland (Home 6–2) and Newcastle United (Home 3–1) in 1920/21 are still a club record. In 1923 came Joe Smith's greatest honour when he was the first FA Cup Final captain to receive the trophy at Wembley. Three years later he lifted the Cup again but his career at Bolton was coming to an end. After heading the Wanderers' league-scoring charts for the sixth time Smith, who had scored 277 goals in 492 games, joined Stockport County in March 1927 for £1,000. For the Edgeley Park club he scored 61 goals in 69 league games, but in 1929 he joined Darwen and had a spell at Manchester Central before becoming manager of Reading. Four years later he became Blackpool's manager, a position he held until April 1958 when he was the longest-serving manager in the Football League. He guided the Seasiders to their best-ever league position and to the 1948, 1951 and 1953 FA Cup Finals.

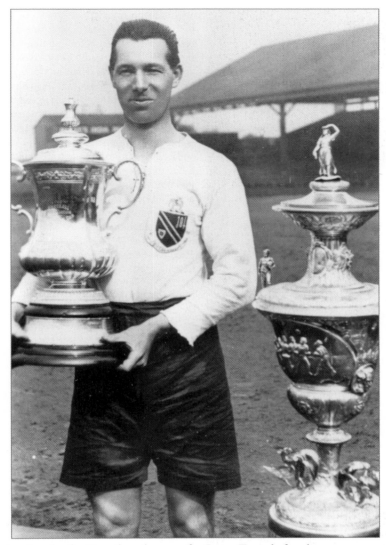

Ted Vizard played rugby for Penarth and soccer for Barry Town before he was recommended to the Wanderers by an old school friend and invited to Burnden for a month's trial. The Wanderers signed him in September 1910 and he made his debut two months later in a 3–0 home win over Gainsborough Trinity. In January 1911, only two months after his Bolton debut, Vizard won the first of his 22 Welsh caps, his last coming in October 1926 when he was 37.

During the First World War Vizard served in the RAF and 'guested' for Chelsea alongside Joe Smith. The pair formed a great left-wing partnership and helped the Pensioners win the 1918 London v. Lancashire Cup Final. In February 1919 the management of Bolton Wanderers was put in Vizard's hands until normal league football returned and Charles Foweraker was appointed. Ted Vizard was a member of Bolton's successful FA Cup-winning teams of 1923 and 1926 and though not a prolific scorer he did score 13 goals in 1925/26, including all three in the 3–0 defeat of Arsenal. He made the last of his 512 League and Cup appearances (during which he scored 70 goals) on 21 March 1931, He was then 41, which makes him the oldest player to appear in a first-team game for the Trotters. He then took charge of the 'A' team before leaving Burnden Park in April 1933 after almost 23 years' service. Vizard became manager of Swindon Town and later took charge of Queen's Park Rangers and Wolverhampton Wanderers.

Sandbach-born forward Frank Roberts played his early football with his home-town teams Sandbach Villa and Sandbach Ramblers before joining Crewe. The Wanderers signed Roberts from the Gresty Road club in May 1914 and after making his debut in a 2–1 win at Bradford City he went on to score 10 goals in 28 games in what was the last season of League football before the First World War. During the first season of peacetime football in 1919/20 Roberts was the club's top scorer, with 26 goals in 40 games, including netting a hat-trick in a 6–3 win at Aston Villa. When Bolton finished third in Division One the following season Roberts formed a prolific partnership with Joe Smith, the two of them scoring 62 of the Wanderers' 77 goals. Roberts had taken his tally of goals to 80 in 168 games when, after being suspended in October 1922, he joined Manchester City. At Maine Road he was the club's leading scorer in 1924/25, 1925/26 and 1927/28 and in 1926 played against Bolton in the FA Cup Final. After helping City win promotion to the First Division in 1927/28 he joined Manchester Central, before ending his career with Horwich RMI.

Jimmy Seddon played his first game for Bolton in February 1914 when he gave away a penalty in a 1–1 draw against Middlesbrough. During the First World War he served in France and contracted trench foot, an affliction that was to trouble him throughout the rest of his career. Seddon didn't turn professional until the summer of 1919 but then was a first team regular for the next 12 seasons, appearing in 375 League and Cup games. He went on to gain three FA Cup winners' medals, captaining the Wanderers in 1929 when they beat Portsmouth 2–0. He won six full caps for England, his first against France in Paris shortly after the Wanderers had beaten West Ham United in the 1923 FA Cup Final. After playing his last game for the Wanderers in January 1932, against Middlesbrough, the team he had made his debut against 18 years earlier, he went as coach to Dordrecht in Holland before holding a similar post with Altrincham. He was later appointed trainer to Southport and then Liverpool Reserves.

CHAPTER THREE

BETWEEN THE WARS

David Jack.

When league football resumed in 1919 the Wanderers appointed Charles Foweraker as their manager, and he became one of the most influential people in the development of the club.

The 1920/21 season saw Bolton make every effort to secure their first-ever League Championship. They broke their record transfer fee in bringing David Jack to Burnden Park but it was Joe Smith, who scored 38 goals in 41 games to equal the Football League record set by Everton's Bert Freeman in 1908, who caught the eye. Sadly the Wanderers lost three of their last 13 games and had to settle for third place, which equalled the club's best-ever position.

However, it was FA Cup football that was to capture the imagination of the Bolton fans in this decade. The Wanderers started the 1922/23 season in disastrous fashion, winning just one of their opening six games, yet by the end of the season they were ensured a permanent place in the history of football with victory in the first-ever FA Cup Final at Wembley. Bolton beat West Ham United 2–0 with goals from David Jack and John Smith, the latter having joined the club earlier in the season from Glasgow Rangers.

Over the next two seasons Bolton came very close to winning the League Championship but finally had to settle for fourth and third place respectively. It could have been so different if the club hadn't made such a poor start to each campaign.

Bolton won the FA Cup again in 1926 when a David Jack goal was enough to beat Manchester City.

The Wanderers made a dreadful start to the 1927/28 season, winning just one of their opening ten games, to find themselves at the foot of Division One for the first time since 1909/10. There followed a remarkable revival which took the club as high as fourth place before results once again went against them and they ended the season in seventh position.

The club won the FA Cup again in 1929, beating Portsmouth 2–0 in the final. Fans were so confident that the Wanderers would succeed that, after their fifth round success over Leicester City, the club received £500-worth of ticket applications for the Wembley final! At one stage that season Bolton had again slumped to the bottom of the League and decided to sell David Jack to Arsenal for what was then a record fee of £10,750. They were then accused of financing the new Burnden Stand with the proceeds from his sale.

It was around this time that players like Dick Pym, Bob Haworth and Ted Vizard came to the end of their League careers but, despite the acquisition of Ray Westwood and Jack Milsom, the Wanderers finally lost their First Division status in 1932/33. They needed to win their final League game of the season at home to Leeds United to stand any chance of staying in the top flight. A hat-trick from Milsom and two goals from Westwood helped Bolton beat their Yorkshire opponents 5–0 but sadly all their rivals also won. That season saw Burnden Park's record attendance, when 69,912 supporters watched the fifth round FA Cup tie against Manchester City which the Maine Road club won 4–2. Unbelievably, four days later the club's lowest crowd for a League game at that time, 3,101, saw them lose 4–1 at home to Portsmouth.

The club missed immediate promotion by one point in 1933/34 but the following season not only won a return to the top flight but established a number of records along the way. The first seven games were all won and the first six victories equalled a feat set in 1899/1900 and created a new club record of 18 games (12 from the previous campaign) without defeat. Wanderers' forward Jack Milsom scored in each of the opening seven games to share the record with the legendary Ted Drake. Also during that 1934/35 season the club recorded their best-ever League victory with an 8-0 demolition of Barnsley with Ray Westwood scoring four of the goals. The Wanderers ended the campaign with 96 goals, the club's highest until 1996/97.

In the seasons up to the outbreak of the Second World War Bolton showed their inconsistency, and in 1935/36 when back in the First Division equalled their worst-ever league defeat when they lost 7–0 at Manchester City. There followed another season of struggle against relegation in 1936/37, but then the last two seasons before the war saw the Wanderers finish seventh and eighth respectively.

Brother of the famous Charles Buchan, Tom Buchan began his Football League career with Blackpool but after playing in 24 first team games for the Seasiders, he joined Bolton and made his debut in October 1914 in a goalless home draw against Everton. Buchan captained the Wanderers throughout the war years, playing in 131 games. He appeared in every position for the club during the hostilities except full-back, even turning out in goal when Bolton lost 4–2 to Stockport County in November 1915. When League football resumed in 1919/20 Buchan was the club's only ever-present as they finished sixth in the First Division. That season he scored a hat-trick as Bolton beat Preston North End 4–1 on Christmas Day. He went on to score 14 goals in 117 League and Cup games before leaving the club in March 1923 to join Tranmere Rovers.

One of the greatest of all Wanderers' wingers, Billy Butler began his career with his home-town club, Atherton, for whom he signed after being demobbed from the army. The Wanderers spotted him playing for Atherton in the Bolton Combination and brought him to Burnden Park in April 1920 where they converted him from centre-forward to outside-right. After making his debut in a 2–0 home defeat by Chelsea, Butler became a virtual ever-present in the Wanderers' side for the next 12 seasons.

He won an England cap against Scotland in 1924, partnering David Jack, and was also the holder of three FA Cup winners' medals in the 1920s, scoring the opening goal in the 1929 final when Bolton beat Portsmouth 2–0.

After the Wanderers were relegated in 1933 Butler asked to go on the transfer list and, having scored 74 goals in 449 League and Cup games, left Burnden Park to join his former team-mate Joe Smith who was manager of Reading. When Smith left to join Blackpool, Butler replaced him as manager of Reading but resigned four years later for personal reasons. He later managed Torquay United before emigrating to South Africa where he coached and managed a number of clubs.

Though David Jack is perhaps most famous for scoring the first goal in a Wembley Cup Final as the Wanderers beat West Ham United 2-0 in 1923, he contributed far more to the game than that. The son of the former Wanderer Bob Jack, he began his Football League career with Plymouth Argyle where his father was manager.

Arsenal and Chelsea with whom he had played during the First World War wanted him, but he chose his home-town club and signed for the Wanderers in December 1920, for a then record fee of £3,500. He made his debut at inside-forward in a goalless draw at Oldham the following month and became a regular thereafter. For the next seven seasons he shared the goalscoring responsibilities with Joe Smith and was the club's top league scorer in five of them, with a best return of 26 goals in 1924/25.

David Jack netted in six of Bolton's seven FA Cup ties on the way to winning the trophy for the first time in 1923. A year later he won the first of four England caps while at Burnden. He scored the winner in the 1926 FA Cup Final but in October 1928, after having scored 161 goals in 324 games, he joined Arsenal for a then record £10,340 transfer and went on to win both League Championship and further FA Cup winners' medals with the Gunners. He later managed Southend United, Middlesbrough and League of Ireland club Shelbourne. He worked as a sportswriter before retiring in April 1955. Jack also worked for the Inland Revenue as he had done in the early part of his career. He died in September 1958.

Bob Haworth became Bolton manager Charles Foweraker's first professional signing when he joined the Wanderers from Atherton Collieries in 1921. Though he had begun his career as a centre-forward, Haworth made his Bolton debut at full-back in a 1–0 win at West Bromwich Albion and held the position virtually unchallenged for the next nine seasons. During that time he was a member of the Bolton side that won the FA Cup three times in the 1920s and after being ever-present in 1929/30 was appointed club captain in place of Jimmy Seddon. He had played in the first 29 games of the season when he broke his leg in Bolton's 4–1 defeat at Grimsby on 17 February 1931. It was his 357th and last appearance for the Wanderers, after which he had a short spell with Accrington Stanley before retiring.

Bolton-born half-back Harry Nuttall made his debut for the Wanderers in a 1–0 home win over FA Cup holders Tottenham Hotspur in September 1921. However, it was midway through the following season before he established himself as a first team regular with the club, ending the campaign with an FA Cup winners' medal after the Wanderers beat West Ham United 2–0 in the first Wembley final. Nuttall in fact was one of four players to win three FA Cup winners' medals in the 1920s as the Wanderers beat Manchester City in 1926 and Portsmouth in 1929. Forming an outstanding half-back line with Seddon and Jennings, he won the first of three caps for England in 1927 when he played in a 2–0 defeat against Ireland.

He played in 326 games for the Wanderers before joining Rochdale in May 1932 but after just one season at Spotland he left to become coach at Nelson. He returned to Burnden Park in 1935 to take up the post of second team trainer, later being responsible for the players' kit and the dressing rooms before retiring in 1964.

Dick Pym, the 'Topsham Fisherman', was born in that Devon village and earned his living from the sea before joining Exeter City in 1911. The Grecians were then members of the Southern League and Pym made 186 consecutive appearances for them before breaking his collarbone in an FA Cup tie against Watford. It was in July 1921 that the Wanderers secured his transfer after weeks of negotiation. Although the precise fee was never revealed, it was thought to be around the £5,000 mark, which was a record for any goalkeeper.

He made his debut in a 2–2 home draw with Preston North End and quickly settled into the team that won the FA Cup in 1923. His qualities were soon recognised and he played for the Football League in Belfast, yet despite his seafaring background he was seasick on the crossing from Liverpool!

In February 1925 he won the first of his three caps for England when he played against Wales at Swansea. He won two more FA Cup winners' medals in 1926 and 1929, keeping a clean sheet in all three Wembley appearances. The last survivor of the 1923 side, Pym played in 336 games for the Wanderers before returning to live in Topsham.

Alex Finney was playing for New Brighton against Chorley in the Lancashire Junior Cup Final at Burnden Park in 1922 when he was noticed by the Wanderers. The Rakers unaccountably forgot to place the full-back's name on the retained list and Bolton lost no time in signing him. After making his debut in a 2–0 defeat at Birmingham in September 1922, he soon established himself in the side and formed a good understanding with right-back Bob Haworth. Finney was the mainstay of the Bolton defence that kept the Hammers at bay in the 1923 FA Cup Final when, at the age of 22, he was the youngest member of the side. In 1923/24 he was the club's only ever-present as they finished fourth in Division One.

A cartilage operation cost Finney his place in the 1926 FA Cup-winning team but he was back for Bolton's 2–0 win over Portsmouth in 1929. In 1928 Finney played for the Football League when they beat the Irish League at Newcastle by 9–1. He played the last of his 530 first team games for the Wanderers on New Year's Day 1937, the last player on the club's books to have played in the Cup Finals of the 1920s.

Signed from Glasgow Rangers as a replacement for Frank Roberts, John Reid Smith played his early football for Albion Rovers, Kilmarnock and Cowdenbeath. He never really settled at Ibrox Park and when Bolton offered £3,000 for his services, he was happy to try his luck south of the border. He scored a last-minute winner on his Bolton debut against Manchester City on 25 November 1922 and at the end of the season scored the club's second goal in the 1923 FA Cup Final win over West Ham United. He continued to be a frequent scorer for the Wanderers and in 1924/25 netted 21 goals in 35 games including a hat-trick in a 4–2 home win over Sheffield United. He scored another treble in the 5–0 win over West Ham at Burnden Park in November 1924 and against Birmingham the following season when the Wanderers won 5–3.

His final hat-trick for the club came in the opening game of the 1926/27 season as Bolton beat Leeds United 5–2 at Elland Road. He had scored 87 goals in 174 games, a total reduced by a series of niggling injuries, when he joined Bury in March 1928. At Bury he scored 108 goals in 157 league games including a hat-trick on his debut.

After beginning his career with Dundee he joined Hamilton Academicals where his brother was on the board. In fact, it was his brother who was instrumental in the inside-forward joining the Wanderers for £3,100 in February 1927. He made his debut in a 1–1 draw against West Bromwich Albion, and in the last ten games of the season he netted nine goals, including his first hat-trick for the club in a 5–0 win over Everton. He remained a first team regular and in 1928/29 scored 20 League and Cup goals including another hat-trick in a 3–1 home win over Sheffield United. Also that season he was a member of the Bolton side that beat Portsmouth 2–0 in the FA Cup Final. His third hat-trick for the club came in February 1920 when Leeds United were beaten 4–2.

Appointed captain in 1931/32, he turned in some outstanding performances as the Wanderers struggled to avoid relegation to the Second Division. The following season the club were relegated but Gibson, who played in the last of his 255 games for Bolton in a 1–1 draw at Chelsea where he scored the Wanderers' goal, left the club in March to join the Stamford Bridge outfit.

After playing his early football for his home-town team of Dundee North End, Willie Cook joined Forfar Athletic before returning to play for Dundee. The left-winger signed for Bolton in December 1928 and on his debut had a hand in all the Wanderers' goals in a 5–0 win over Leicester City. At the end of his first season with the club he won an FA Cup winners' medal as Bolton beat Portsmouth 2–0 in the Wembley final.

Capped three times by Scotland during his time with the Wanderers, he helped the club win promotion to the First Division in 1934/35 following their relegation two seasons earlier, but after just one season back in the top flight he left Burnden Park to play for Blackpool. Cook, who scored 40 goals in 262 games, helped the Seasiders win promotion to the First Division in his first season at Bloomfield Road before returning to his native Scotland to end his career with Dundee.

Scotsman Billy McKay joined the Wanderers from Hamilton Academicals in December 1929 and made his debut in a 1–1 draw against Manchester United at Old Trafford. However, he failed to establish himself in the Bolton side in the five seasons he spent with the club, his highest number of League appearances being 28 in 1930/31. Though he was moved from inside-forward to wing-half in 1932, it was to no avail, for at the end of the 1932/33 season the club were relegated to the Second Division.

After being placed on the transfer list McKay, who had scored 17 goals in 109 games, signed for Manchester United. He helped the Reds win the Second Division Championship in 1935/36 and then following immediate relegation finish in the runners-up spot in the same division in 1937/38. He scored 15 goals in 184 games for United before leaving to play non-league football with Stalybridge Celtic.

Harold Blackmore joined Bolton Wanderers in unusual circumstances: the Burnden Park club had visited Exeter City to play the Grecians in Robert Pollard's benefit game and lost 3–2, Blackmore scoring two of Exeter's goals. Immediately after the game the Wanderers paid £2,150 to bring Blackmore to Burnden Park, the Silverton-born forward having scored 44 goals in 74 games.

He made his Bolton debut in April 1927, scoring in a 3–2 win over Sheffield Wednesday. The following season he scored eight goals in 12 games including four in a 7–1 home win over Burnley, but it wasn't until 1928/29 that he won a regular place in the Wanderers' side. That season he was the club's leading scorer with 37 goals in 43 League and Cup games including hat-tricks against Portsmouth (Home 4–2), Aston Villa (Away 5–3), Birmingham (Home 6–2) and the second goal in the FA Cup Final victory over Portsmouth at Wembley. He also headed the Wanderers' goalscoring charts in 1929/30 with 30 goals, four of which came in a 5–0 win over Everton and in 1930/31 when a similar total included him finding the net in seven successive games. He had scored 122 goals in 165 games before later playing for Middlesbrough, Badford and Bury.

Bedminster-born centre-forward Jack Milsom had short spells with Bristol Rovers and Kettering Town before joining Rochdale in the summer of 1928. In his first season at Spotland he scored 25 goals, and this prompted Bolton to pay £1,750 in December 1929, to take him to Burnden Park.

Despite scoring on his debut in a 4–2 win over Leeds United and netting six goals in a Central League game against Wolverhampton Wanderers he could not force his way into the Bolton side on a regular basis. Just when it seemed he would be given an extended run in the side he broke his leg and had to wait until 1931/32 before becoming an established first team player. He was the club's leading scorer for the next six seasons with a best of 35 goals in 46 games during the Wanderers' promotion-winning season of 1934/35.

The scorer of nine hat-tricks, he also scored four goals against Liverpool in an 8–1 win for the Wanderers on the final day of the 1931/32 season and against West Ham (1933/34) and Burnley (1934/35). He had scored 153 goals in 255 games when he left Bolton in February 1938 to end his career with Manchester City.

Harry Goslin was one of the game's true gentlemen and a great leader. He joined the Wanderers in August 1930 for a £25 donation to Nottingham club Boots Athletic. He made his debut in a 7–2 defeat at Liverpool but kept his place in the side for the remainder of the season. After that he missed very few games and was ever-present in 1934/35, when the Wanderers won promotion to the First Division, and 1938/39. When Alex Finney left the club, Goslin was appointed captain, a position he held up to the outbreak of the Second World War when he had scored 23 goals in 334 games.

During the war he 'guested' for Chelsea and Norwich City and won selection for England's wartime team. He was killed in the Italian campaign on 18 December 1943 when serving with the 53rd Field Regiment RA (Bolton Artillery) with which he had also fought in Africa and France.

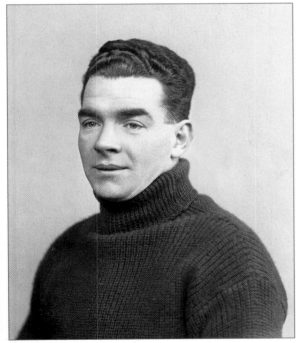

Liverpool-born goalkeeper Bob Jones began his Football League career with Everton before joining Southport. He arrived at Burnden Park in March 1929 and made his debut in a 3–1 defeat at Birmingham. After that he missed very few matches and was ever-present in 1931/32. He had played in 77 consecutive league matches for the Wanderers when he was laid low by appendicitis.

In 1934/35 Jones was in outstanding form as Bolton won promotion to the First Division and reached the FA Cup semi-final where they lost 2–0 to West Bromwich Albion after a replay. Jones went on to appear in 244 games for the Wanderers before leaving to end his League career with Cardiff City. In 1939 he returned to Haig Avenue as Southport's assistant trainer and after the Second World War spent eight seasons with the Sandgrounders as first team trainer.

George Eastham made his Bolton debut at Blackpool's Bloomfield Road ground on 1 April 1933, and though the Wanderers won 3–1 that day they lost their next three games and were relegated to the Second Division. It was midway through the following season before Eastham established himself in the Bolton side. In 1934/35 he helped the Wanderers reach the semi-finals of the FA Cup and win promotion to the First Division, his form earning him his only international cap when he played in England's 1–0 win over Holland in Amsterdam.

He went on to score 17 goals in 131 games before joining Brentford for a fee of £4,500. A little over a year later he returned to the north-west to play for Blackpool. During the Second World War he and his brother Harry 'guested' for the Wanderers. After spells with Swansea, Rochdale and Lincoln he became player-manager of Irish League side Ards before taking charge at Accrington Stanley. After just one season he returned to Ireland to manage both Distillery and Ards, later having a spell as coach and assistant-manager of Stoke City.

Captain of the England schoolboys, George Taylor signed for the Wanderers in a disused tramcar in a tramshed where his father worked. Though he made his Bolton debut in a 3–3 draw at Blackpool in February 1931, it was 1933/34 before he began to establish himself as a first team regular because a broken ankle had kept him out of the entire 1932/33 campaign.

In 1934/35 Taylor missed just one game as the Wanderers were promoted and the following season after some impressive performances in the top flight, he was chosen as a reserve for the England team. He had appeared in 244 League and Cup games for Bolton when the war interrupted his career, though he did turn out in 75 wartime games for the club before hanging up his boots. Taylor was later appointed chief coach, a position he held when the Wanderers won the FA Cup in 1958. Even when he had retired he still worked for the club on a part-time basis, thus serving Bolton in a variety of capacities for over 50 years.

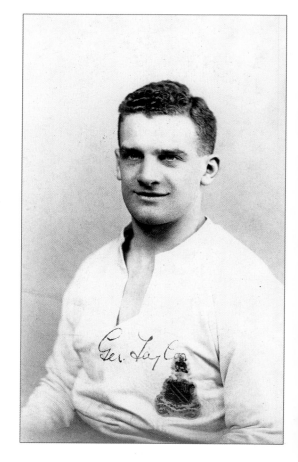

Ray Westwood played his early football with Stourbridge and Brierley Hill Alliance before having a trial with Aston Villa. Fortunately for the Wanderers this came to nothing, and on the recommendation of former centre-half Jack Round the Wanderers secured his services on amateur forms in the summer of 1928. He turned professional in March 1931 and made his first team debut in a 1–1 home draw against Manchester City. Forming a formidable partnership with Willie Cook, Westwood's performances led to him representing the Football League and winning six full caps for England, the first against Wales in September 1934.

In 1934/35, when the Wanderers finished runners-up to Brentford in the Second Division and so won promotion to the top flight, Westwood scored 30 goals in 38 League games, including four in the 8–0 home win over Barnsley, all of his goals coming in the first 39 minutes of the match. During the 1937/38 season when the Wanderers finished seventh in Division One, Westwood was the club's top scorer with 23 goals in 33 League games, including hat-tricks against Chelsea (Home 5–5) and Grimsby Town (Home 3–1). He continued to play for the Wanderers after the Second World War, taking his tally of goals to 144 in 333 League and Cup games before moving to join Chester. After ending his career with Darwen, he returned to his home town Brierley Hill and became a newsagent.

Though Horwich-born winger Tom Woodward played his first game for the Wanderers as an 18-year-old at home to Stoke in February 1936, it was another two years before he played again. In 1938/39 he shared the wing role with Albert Geldard, scoring three goals in 24 League games. During the war years he appeared in 118 games for the club, including being an ever-present in 1944/45 when the Wanderers won the Football League North Cup.

He missed very few games when League football resumed but in October 1949, after he had scored 19 goals in 169 League and Cup games, he joined Middlesbrough for a fee of £7,500. His first game for the Teesside club was at Burnden Park, scoring Middlesbrough's first goal in a 2–1 win for the Ayresome Park club. However, his stay in the north-east was brief and he returned to the area to see out his career with Wigan Athletic.

A former England schoolboy international, George Thomas Taylor began his Football League career with Notts County, a First Division side at the time of his debut in 1925. Despite two seasons of relegation Taylor missed very few games and was ever-present when the Meadow Lane club regained their Second Division status in 1931/32. He had played in 265 League games for County when Bolton paid £3,500 for his services in December 1933. Known to the fans as 'GT' so as not to confuse him with the club's other George Taylor, he made his debut in a 2–1 home win over Swansea Town. After that he played in 132 consecutive games for the Wanderers before injury forced him to miss the game against Derby County in October 1936. The tricky winger went on to score 29 goals in 170 League and Cup games before joining Coventry City, where he ended his League career after 65 appearances for the Highfield Road club.

Loyal one-club man Don Howe worked on the groundstaff at Burnden Park before, shortly after signing professional forms, he was given his first team debut in a goalless draw at Liverpool in October 1936. Until the outbreak of the Second World War Howe played in every position for the club except centre-forward, and in 1938/39 had his best season for the Wanderers in terms of goals scored when he found the net on nine occasions. During the hostilities Howe 'guested' for Newcastle United and Norwich City. On his return to Burnden Park Howe played the majority of his games at wing-half and was appointed club captain. An ever-present in 1950/51, Howe went on to score 35 goals in 286 League and Cup games before retiring from the game in the summer of 1952. Howe, who had qualified as an FA coach, was given the opportunity to work with the Bolton 'B' team but he opted to leave the game completely and went to work for a local firm of paper merchants.

Jack Atkinson was spotted by Bolton playing for Washington Colliery in his native County Durham and though the Wanderers immediately signed the resolute defender, he was allowed to continue playing for his old club in a forward position in an attempt to speed him up. Though Atkinson didn't cost a fee, the Wanderers made a number of donations to the Colliery club's funds.

He arrived at Burnden Park in the summer of 1931, and after playing centre-half for the 'A' team and reserves he made his first team debut in a 2–2 draw at home to West Bromwich Albion in April 1933. Bolton's regular centre-half Tom Griffiths had signed for Middlesbrough and so Atkinson became the club's first choice pivot, turning in a number of impressive performances that were unlucky not to win him international recognition. During the Second World War he 'guested' for Blackpool and Everton as well as playing in 74 wartime games for the Wanderers. He continued to serve the club after the hostilities and was the regular centre-half for the 1946/47 season, but midway through the following campaign he lost his place to Lol Hamlett. In April 1948 after playing in 263 League and Cup games he joined New Brighton as player-manager.

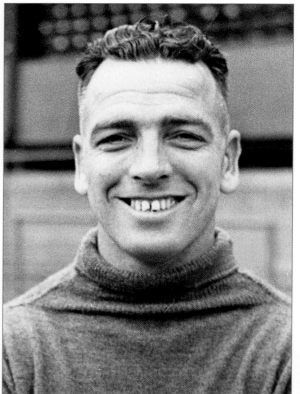

Goalkeeper Stan Hanson, famed for his long-distance kicking, had amateur experience with both Liverpool and Southport before turning down overtures from Aston Villa and signing for the Wanderers. He made his debut in a 2–0 defeat at Huddersfield Town in September 1936 but it wasn't until the 1938/39 season that he established himself as the club's first-choice custodian.

During the Second World War he appeared for the Eighth Army in their 4–2 win over Yugoslavia. When League football resumed in 1946/47 Hanson was ever-present and missed very few games over the next nine seasons, being ever-present again in 1950/51 and 1952/53. His consistency was rewarded when in 1950 he toured Canada with the FA. Hanson was in the Bolton goal in the 'Matthews Final' in 1953 when the Wanderers lost 4–3 to Blackpool. He stayed with the Wanderers until 1955, his 40th year, when after 423 appearances he was given a free transfer. He then played part-time for Rhyl before running the Burnden Post Office opposite the ground.

Swansea-born John Roberts was one of the few players to represent the Wanderers on either side of the Second World War. He joined Bolton in April 1936 from Cwmburia but had to wait almost two years before making his first team debut in a 1–1 home draw against Sunderland on 19 February 1938. It was his only appearance that season but in 1938/39 he scored eight goals in 17 games from his position at inside-forward, including a hat-trick in a 4–2 win over Everton.

During the war he 'guested' for Norwich City but on his return to Burnden Park he was switched to right-back and was a virtual ever-present for the next four seasons. His form was such that he was made captain and in May 1949 he was capped by Wales at full international level when he played against Belgium. He had appeared in 171 League and Cup games for Bolton when he returned to play for his home-town club in September 1950, later playing non-league football for Llanelli.

CHAPTER FOUR

NAT LOFTHOUSE

Lofthouse in action.

Whenever football conversation turns to 'real' centre-forwards, then there is one name that is certain to be mentioned – Nat Lofthouse. He was big and strong just as most centre-forwards were supposed to be but in the age of the maximum wage he was also loyal to his only club, Bolton Wanderers. He was proud of his ability and status but always remained a member of the local community.

Nathaniel Lofthouse was Bolton born (27 August 1925) and Bolton bred. His father was head horsekeeper for Bolton Corporation and Nat was the youngest of four sons. His first proper game of football was not a happy one; pressed into service as an emergency goalkeeper, the 11-year-old debutant suffered the indignity of picking the ball out of the net seven times! But that match gave him an insight into what organised football was all about and on his own request he was included in the school team – at centre-forward. Size was the determining factor then, but he made steady progress and when he earned his debut for the Bolton Schools XI against Bury, the neighbouring team were hammered 7–1 – and Lofthouse scored all seven!

It was the Mayor of Bolton himself, a Bolton director, who asked him to join the Wanderers. He was signed as a 14-year-old amateur in 1939 and made his first team debut in 1940. Bury were again the victims, though this time Lofthouse was content with only a brace of goals. Professional terms were the reward – £1 10s per match, plus 2s 6d expenses – Nat's childhood ambition to make the grade with Bolton Wanderers was fulfilled.

He still had to prove himself. Wartime football was not easy. Bevin Boy Lofthouse's Saturdays went like this: up at 3.30 a.m., catching the 4.30 tram to work; eight hours down the pit pushing tubs; collected by the team coach; playing for Bolton. But work down the mine toughened him physically and the caustic humour of his fellow miners made sure he never became arrogant about his success on the field.

When the war finished the chance to play alongside established professionals returning from the forces gave Lofthouse the final confidence he needed and he was a regular in the league side from the resumption in 1946.

Goals flowed regularly, attracting favourable press comment as it became obvious that Lofthouse had international potential.

In 1949 he scored four goals for the FA XI against the Army – three from pin-point Stanley Matthews' crosses – and in the following year he was selected for the FA's summer tour of Canada.

The call to full international honours came the following November against Yugoslavia. The game was played at Highbury and despite the presence of ex-ballet dancer Beara in goal and 6ft 4in Horvath at centre-half, both England goals in the 2–2 draw were scored by Lofthouse. Within a year he was established as England's centre-forward and from October 1951 to November 1953 he did not miss a single game for his country. One of those 18 matches against Austria in May 1952 was to give Lofthouse the famous nickname 'Lion of Vienna'.

Before a capacity crowd of 65,000 in the Prater Stadium, the stage was set for a match that both sides desperately wanted to win. Austria began with a series of furious attacks. Lofthouse scored, Huber equalised and the stadium erupted. Sewell restored England's lead. Hysterical scenes greeted Austria's second equaliser scored by Dienst. Austria attacked with renewed frenzy but to no avail. One raid ended when England goalkeeper Gil Merrick plucked the ball off Dienst's head and threw it upfield to Tom Finney. Finney's shrewd through ball put Lofthouse clear. With the desperate defence in pounding pursuit, Lofthouse slid the ball under the advancing Musil before being felled by a crunching tackle. It was a great triumph but as he regretfully said: 'I never saw the ball enter the Austrian net for the best goal of my life'.

Strangely, his international career seemed to be over after the 1955/56 season, one of his best – 32 league goals in 36 games including four in a 6–0 win over Birmingham City and four international goals in five games. The 1958 World Cup came and went, then Lofthouse was surprisingly recalled to the England team for two games and scored his 30th international goal (equalling Tom Finney's newly established record) with a powerful shot against Russia.

During this fine international career, Lofthouse remained content to play for Bolton. He was a classic example of the loyal club man under the maximum wage system; proud to play for the same club for 15 seasons.

Lofthouse earned £15 a week. His bread and butter League scoring consistency, coupled with his international success, brought him the accolade of Footballer of the Year in 1953 – the trophy being presented the night before the Cup Final in which Bolton were beaten 4–3 by Blackpool. Lofthouse took to the pitch needing a goal to complete a remarkable record of scoring in every round. He did not have to wait long, for within two minutes a long crossfield pass found Holden on the right wing. His quick inside pass found Lofthouse, who hit the ball home from 25 yards. It was 1958 before Lofthouse gained an FA Cup winners' medal as Bolton beat Manchester United 2–0. He scored both goals that day – the second seeing Manchester United goalkeeper Harry Gregg hit the net as hard as the ball after Lofthouse's charge caught him off the ground.

Before nagging injury ended his playing career in the early 1960s, he had scored over 300 goals – 255 in 452 League games, 30 in 51 Cup games, 30 in 33 internationals, and he even scored a hat-trick in each half for the Football League against the League of Ireland at Molineux.

After a spell out of the game, when he kept a pub, he returned to the Wanderers in 1968 as manager. The experiment was not a success and though he was replaced briefly he was then re-appointed. He left the club in 1971 on Jimmy Armfield's appointment but returned to become executive club manager and later president to continue his devotion to Lancashire's oldest club.

Nat receives his OBE at Buckingham Palace.

Nat on his wedding day – 6 December 1947. A few hours later he was playing for Bolton v. Wolves at Burnden Park and scoring twice in a 3–2 win!

Nat in action for the Wanderers against Sheffield Wednesday.

Nat lifts the FA Cup aloft after the Wanderers had beaten Manchester United 2–0 in the 1958 FA Cup Final. He is surrounded by Brian Birch, Eddie Hopkinson and Derek Hennin.

Nat's last appearance for England in a 5–0 win over Russia at Wembley during which he scored his thirtieth international goal.

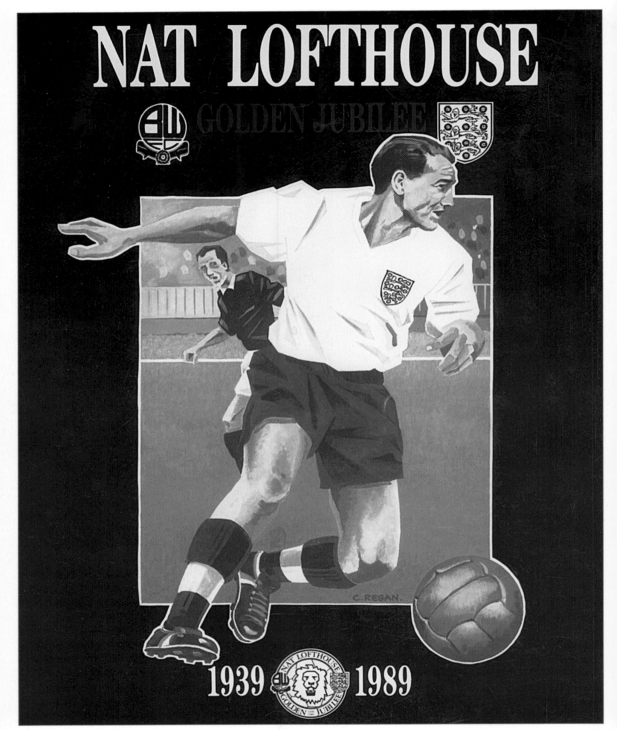

Nat Lofthouse's Golden Jubilee official souvenir programme cover to commemorate the fiftieth anniversary of the day 'Lofty' signed for the Wanderers.

CHAPTER FIVE
1946–1999

Tragedy at Burnden Park, 1946.

The early seasons after the Second World War were somewhat disappointing though the club did win the Lancashire Cup in 1948 and Willie Moir, who scored a hat-trick in that final, was the First Division's leading scorer in 1948/49 with 25 goals.

With Bill Ridding appointed as manager, the Wanderers set the pace in the First Division in 1951/52 but ended in fifth place, nine points adrift of champions Manchester United. The following season saw Bolton reach the FA Cup Final at Wembley with Nat Lofthouse scoring in every round. Not surprisingly, come Cup Final week, 'Lofty' was named Footballer of the Year. In the final the Wanderers led 3–1, but in what became known as the 'Matthews' Final' Blackpool ran out 4–3 winners.

Undismayed by this reverse, Bolton mounted a concerted challenge for League and Cup honours in 1953/54, finishing fifth in the First Division and reaching the quarter-finals of the FA Cup.

The following season the Reserves won the Central League title for the only time in the club's history and the Wanderers' youngsters reached the semi-finals of the FA Youth Cup.

However, it was in the FA Cup that the Wanderers tasted success in 1958. The team put together by Bill Ridding and had cost nothing but signing-on fees beat Manchester United 2–0 with Lofthouse scoring both goals. The first came after a couple of minutes and the second, one of the most controversial goals in Cup Final history, saw Lofty charge both the ball and the United 'keeper Harry Gregg over the goal-line.

After beating Wolves 4–1 in the FA Charity Shield, Bolton ended the 1958/59 season in fourth place in Division One and reached the quarter-finals of the FA Cup. The following season saw the Wanderers playing without the services of Nat Lofthouse who turned his ankle in pre-season training and missed the whole of the campaign, yet they still finished in sixth position.

After coming close to relegation in 1962/63 Bolton started the 1963/64 campaign with five straight League defeats. In fact, they won only three matches before Christmas, two of them against bottom club, Ipswich Town. When the last game of the season arrived Bolton needed to beat Wolves but lost 4–0 and were relegated.

In 1964/65 the Wanderers were in the promotion hunt for most of the season, but sadly after scoring only twice in their last five games they finished third behind Newcastle United and Northampton Town. They then spent the rest of the decade fighting to stave off relegation to the Third Division.

In 1970/71 the Wanderers finally lost their place in the Second Division, ending the season at the foot of the table with just 24 points. New manager Jimmy Armfield set about remedying the situation and in 1972/73 the club returned to the Second

Division as champions of Division Three. After re-establishing the club in the Second Division, Armfield left to manage Leeds and was replaced by Ian Greaves.

He took the Wanderers to a League Cup semi-final appearance and to within a whisker of promotion to the top flight on two occasions before the club won the Second Division Championship in 1977/78. After finishing seventeenth in the First Division in 1978/79 with Frank Worthington topping the divisional scoring charts, the club had high hopes for 1979/80, but despite a number of big money buys the Wanderers still finished bottom of the league and were relegated.

After three seasons of struggle the Wanderers were relegated to the Third Division, losing their last game of the 1982/83 season 4–1 at Charlton Athletic, the same result on the same ground as the first time the club were relegated to Division Three.

In 1986 Phil Neal took the Wanderers to Wembley but they lost 3–0 to Bristol City in the Freight Rover Trophy Final. The following season the club finished in a relegation play-off place, and after losing to Aldershot entered the Fourth Division for the first time in their history.

The Wanderers won promotion at the first attempt after a Robbie Savage goal gave them a 1–0 win at Wrexham on the final day of the season.

In 1989 the Wanderers returned to Wembley and beat Torquay United 4–1 to win the Sherpa Van Trophy. The following season in Bolton finished sixth but lost to Notts County in the play-offs, while after finishing fourth in 1990/91 they beat Bury before losing 1–0 to Tranmere Rovers in the play-off final at Wembley.

It was 1992/93 when the Wanderers finally won promotion as runners-up to Stoke City after losing only one of their last 19 games and in the course of the season beat Liverpool at Anfield after the first match at Burnden had been drawn. The following season Bolton reached the sixth round of the FA Cup, beating Premier League opposition in Everton, Arsenal and Aston Villa before losing to Oldham Athletic.

The 1994/95 season saw the Wanderers win through to the Coca Cola Cup Final at Wembley where Alan Thompson scored Bolton's goal in a 2–1 defeat by Liverpool. In the League, Bolton finished third and after beating Wolves in the play-off semi-finals defeated Reading 4–3 after extra time in the Wembley final.

Sadly the Wanderers found the transition from Division One to Premiership difficult and ended their first season in bottom place, nine points adrift of safety.

In 1996/97 the club's last season at Burnden Park, the Wanderers won the First Division Championship in style, scoring 100 goals and securing 98 points, 18 more than runners-up Barnsley.

Despite moving to the new Reebok Stadium, the Wanderers endured another season of struggle and though a result at Chelsea on the final day of the season would have seen them to safety they couldn't raise themselves sufficiently and lost 2–0.

It was on the afternoon of 9 March 1946 that Burnden Park became the scene of one of the worst disasters the English game has known, yet though 33 people were killed many people present at the game were unaware of the tragedy. An estimated 85,000 crowd had poured into Burnden Park – the official 'gate' figure is only 65,419 – for the second leg of an FA Cup sixth round tie against Stoke City.

The crowd was so tightly packed that many spectators tried to get out of the ground. As the pressure mounted, two crash barriers collapsed. Spectators were hurtled forward and many were trampled underfoot. Dead and wounded were laid out on the running track, doctors being summoned from the crowd to attend to them. The game was just 12 minutes old when the referee was informed of the full extent of the tragedy. He took the players off the field, but after consultation with the police play was resumed after a 12-minute break. It was felt that this was the wisest decision. Play continued until its finish with no interval being taken. In addition to the 33 fatalities 500 were injured, 24 of whom were taken to hospital. The Mayor of Bolton opened a Relief Fund and a total of almost £40,000 was raised. The match itself ended in a 0–0 draw, so Bolton having won the first leg 2–0 went through to the semi-finals.

The skilful Scot joined the Wanderers in 1943 after being spotted playing for the RAF team at Kirkham by Bolton's chief scout, Bob Jackson. During the war years he 'guested' for both Aberdeen and Dundee and in 1945 played for Bolton in the North v. South Cup Final.

When league football resumed after the hostilities Moir, who was predominantly right-footed, played most of his football at outside-left after having made his league debut in a 4–3 defeat at Chelsea on the opening day of the 1946/47 season. However, at the beginning of the 1948/49 season he was switched to inside-right and scored all four goals including a penalty in a 4–2 win at Aston Villa. He was ever-present that season and ended the campaign as the First Division's leading scorer with 25 goals, a total which included another four-goal haul in a 6–1 win over Sheffield United and a hat-trick in a 4–1 defeat of Middlesbrough. Forming an ideal partnership with Nat Lofthouse, Moir continued to find the net, his form winning him international recognition when he played for Scotland against England in April 1950. He had scored 134 goals in 358 games when he left to become player-manager of Stockport County.

Malcolm Barrass was the son of a former professional, his father Matt having played for Blackpool, Sheffield Wednesday and Manchester City. Having turned down Wolves, he signed for Bolton in November 1944 and during the wartime competition played for the Wanderers at centre-forward, scoring 30 goals in 68 games. His performances led to him playing for England in the Victory international against Wales at the Hawthorns.

When League football resumed, he showed his versatility by playing in a number of positions and in one game against Manchester City in November 1948 he wore the number nine shirt and scored four goals in a 5–1 win. Eventually he reverted to centre-half, and that was the position in which he won his three full caps for England and in which he appeared against Blackpool in the 1953 FA Cup Final. After 12 years with the Wanderers in which he scored 27 goals in 357 League and Cup games, he joined Sheffield United in September 1956, later becoming player-manager of non-league Wigan Athletic. He eventually ended his playing career in the Southern League with Nuneaton Borough.

Farnworth-born left-back Tommy Banks was one of the 'hard men' of the Bolton side during the 1950s; tales of opposition wingers who were deposited on the cinder track being only part of the story of this England international. On his arrival at Burnden Park he found his first team opportunities limited by his older brother Ralph, who occupied one of the full-back berths. Despite making his League debut in a 1–0 defeat at Wolves in April 1948, it was to be 1953/54 before he won a regular place in the side, Banks making just 12 appearances in his first five seasons with the club.

It was towards the end of his Bolton career that Banks reached his peak. After winning an FA Cup medal against Manchester United in May 1958 he won the first of six England caps when he played against Russia in Moscow. He later played in the World Cup Finals in Sweden. Banks, who was the subject of an inquiry by Manchester United during their rebuilding after the Munich air disaster, played in 265 games for the Wanderers before leaving to join non-league Altrincham in 1961. He later left the game to concentrate on the building trade.

Yorkshireman Bryan Edwards made his Bolton debut in a 3–3 draw at Liverpool in September 1950 and later that season became a regular in the Wanderers' side. Two years later he was called up for National Service, and this not only prevented him from playing on a regular basis and cost his place in the 1953 FA Cup Final team but also prevented him from beating the Trotters' appearance record then held by Alex Finney. He regained his first team spot from Eric Bell at the start of the 1954/55 season and over the next five seasons missed just six games, culminating in him collecting an FA Cup winners' medal in 1958 when Bolton beat Manchester United 2–0. It was Edwards' pass that was deflected into the path of Nat Lofthouse to open the scoring after two minutes.

Edwards, whose experience in the latter years of his Bolton career proved invaluable to young wing-halves Warwick Rimmer and Graham Stanley, appeared in 518 League and Cup games. After leaving Bolton, he coached at Blackpool, Preston and Plymouth, then managed Bradford City before serving Huddersfield, Leeds and Bradford City again in a variety of roles, including physiotherapist.

Having previously played with Prescot Cables, England youth international Derek Hennin made his debut for the Wanderers as a replacement for the injured Johnny Wheeler in a 3–2 defeat at Tottenham Hotspur in March 1954. He held his place for the remaining 11 games of the season as the Whites ended the campaign in fifth place in Division One.

Hennin then returned to the reserves and helped them win the Central League title in 1955. It wasn't until Wheeler left to join Liverpool in 1957 that Hennin established himself as a first team regular and over the next five seasons appeared in 183 games for the club.

In April 1958 the versatile Hennin turned out as an emergency centre-forward for the Wanderers' Good Friday game at home to Aston Villa. He scored a hat-trick in a 4–0 win for Bolton with one of his goals coming from the penalty spot. He picked up an FA Cup winners' medal in 1958, but after losing his first team place to Graham Stanley he left Burnden Park in 1962 to join Chester. He later played non-league football for Wigan Athletic.

Bobby Langton played his early football for Southport League side Burscough Victoria before joining Blackburn Rovers in 1937. Quickly installed into the inside-left position he scored 14 goals in 37 games during Rovers' promotion campaign of 1938/39. On his return to Ewood Park after the war he won his first cap for England, but in August 1948 he was transferred to Preston North End for £16,000. After only 15 months at Deepdale, Langton was on his way to Bolton Wanderers for what was then a club record fee of £20,000.

He made his debut in a 3–0 home win over Manchester City and was a regular in the club's number eleven shirt until the end of the 1952/53 season when he was placed on the transfer list at his own request. He remained long enough to play in the 1953 FA Cup Final against Blackpool but having scored 18 goals in 132 games he returned to Ewood Park. In his second spell with Rovers he took his total of goals to 57 in 212 League games before later playing for Ards, Kidderminster Harriers, Wisbech Town and Colwyn Bay. He later returned to his roots to manage Burscough Rangers.

In his early days with the Wanderers John Higgins was a full-back, but while doing his National Service he developed into a fine centre-half. Though he made his debut for the injured Malcolm Barrass in a 1–0 win at Burnley in March 1953, it wasn't until 1956/57 that he established himself as a first team regular.

He was at his best in 1957/58 when he was the club's vice-captain and the only ever-present in a season when the Wanderers won the FA Cup. In fact, he captained the side in the absence of Nat Lofthouse in the FA Cup semi-final when Wanderers beat Blackburn Rovers 2–1 at Maine Road. Standing 6 feet plus and weighing 14 stone, Higgins' strength was an important factor in the Wanderers twice finishing in the top six of the First Division during his time with the club. In February 1960 he became the first Bolton player to be dismissed in a Football League game since the war when he was sent off at Hillsborough in a 1–0 defeat by Sheffield Wednesday. He went on to appear in 202 games for the Wanderers before joining non-league Wigan Athletic and later becoming general manager of Stockport County.

Doug Holden signed as an amateur for the Wanderers in 1948 and appeared for the England Youth side before completing his National Service. He made his League debut in a 1–1 draw against Liverpool at Anfield in November 1951, and though he was only 17 he quickly proved that he possessed the temperament for the big occasion. Holden in fact had only made 12 Central League appearances before his promotion to the first team. Though he played primarily on the left flank, it was on the opposite wing that he made a name for himself in the 1953 FA Cup Final.

Five years later he reverted to the left wing for the 1958 FA Cup Final against Manchester United – he and Lofthouse being the only Bolton players to appear in both finals. In March 1959 he played for the Football League against the Irish League in Dublin. Impressing in that match, he was selected for the full England side against Scotland at Wembley. In November 1962, after scoring 44 goals in 463 games for the Wanderers, he left to join Preston North End for whom he appeared in the 1964 FA Cup Final. He later emigrated to Australia and played for the national side.

Liverpool-born wing-half Johnny Wheeler was Bill Ridding's first signing when he joined the Wanderers from Tranmere Rovers in February 1951. He made his debut in a 2–1 home win over Liverpool and then held his place virtually unchallenged for the next five seasons. On 3 January 1953 he was asked to play as an emergency centre-forward and responded with a hat-trick in a 4–0 win over Blackpool.

After winning Football League and England 'B' honours, he won his only full cap for his country when in October 1954 he played against Northern Ireland in Belfast. He went on to score 18 goals in 205 games for the Wanderers before rather surprisingly being released to join his cousin Ronnie Moran at Liverpool. He made 164 League appearances for the Anfield club before taking up the post of assistant trainer at Bury.

A cousin of the great Duncan Edwards, Dennis Stevens made his Bolton debut in a 3–1 defeat at Preston North End in September 1953 though it was 1955/56 before he became a regular following the retirement of Harold Hassall. He continued to make steady progress and won selection for both the Football League and England Under-23s, though a full cap continued to elude him, despite being called into Walter Winterbottom's squad in 1957. A year later Stevens won an FA Cup winners' medal when Wanderers beat Manchester United 2–0 at Wembley.

His best season for Bolton in terms of goals scored was 1959/60 when Nat Lofthouse was injured, Stevens finding the net 15 times. He had scored 101 goals in 310 games when in March 1962 he was allowed to join Everton for £35,000. Playing in a much deeper role, he helped the Blues win the League Championship in 1962/63 but after scoring 21 goals in 130 games joined Oldham Athletic before ending his career with Tranmere Rovers.

When Ray Parry made his Bolton debut against Wolverhampton Wanderers at Molineux on 13 October 1951, he became the youngest player in First Division history at 15 years 267 days. The Derby-born youngster was only given two outings that season before gradually settling into the side at inside-forward. One of a famous footballing family, Ray Parry developed into a player who could pass the ball with great accuracy and yet could strike it with great power. He was the scorer of some vital goals, perhaps none more so than the one against Wolves in the FA Cup sixth round tie of 1958. A member of that season's FA Cup-winning side, he also won two caps for England, scoring in a 2–1 win over Northern Ireland on his international debut.

He had scored 79 goals in 299 games for the Wanderers when in October 1960 he was transferred to Blackpool for £25,000. After four years at Bloomfield Road, he moved to Bury where he made his debut against Bolton. He remained with the Shakers until 1972 before ending his playing career with non-league New Brighton.

Signed from Bromsgrove Rovers, full-back Roy Hartle made his Bolton debut in a 2–1 defeat at home to Charlton Athletic on New Year's Day 1953. Despite the reversal, Hartle had impressed and kept his place in the side for the next 24 games which included seven matches in the club's run to the FA Cup Final at Wembley. He was devastated when he was dropped in favour of John Ball for the showpiece against Blackpool.

However, after completing his National Service he returned to win a regular place in the team and form with Tommy Banks the most feared full-back pairing in the Football League! Hartle was a virtual ever-present in the Wanderers side for the next 11 seasons, often captaining the side. He won an FA Cup winners' medal in 1958 and was considered unlucky not to gain international recognition. He had played in 499 League and Cup games for the club when he left to end his playing career with non-league Buxton of the Cheshire League. Hartle, who served on the executive of the PFA, also spent a year coaching NASL side New York Generals before becoming chief scout at Bury.

The holder of the club's appearance record with 578 first team outings between 1956 and 1969, Eddie Hopkinson remains the best goalkeeper the Wanderers have ever had. He became a 'naturalised' Lancastrian when his family moved south from Durham to Royton near Oldham. He soon signed as an amateur for Oldham Athletic and was only 16 years of age when he played in three Third Division (North) games in 1951/52. At the end of that season the Latics overlooked him to Bolton's lasting satisfaction. He joined the Wanderers in August 1952, signing professional forms the following November.

His meteoric rise began in 1956 when Bolton's regular 'keeper Ken Grieves couldn't be released from his cricketing duties as Lancashire were chasing Championship honours. Eddie got his chance in the senior side against Blackpool which the Wanderers won 4–1 and went through a brilliant first season without missing a game. In summer 1957 he was awarded the first of six England Under-23 caps on a tour behind the Iron Curtain. In October of that year he made his first full international appearance against Northern Ireland, going on to win 14 caps.

In 1958 he kept a clean sheet to win an FA Cup winners' medal as the Wanderers beat Manchester United 2–0 at Wembley. At Norwich City in January 1969 he broke Bolton's long-standing appearance record set by Alex Finney and but for an injury which kept him out of the side for most of the 1958/59 season and another which put him out of action for a 10-match spell in 1963/64, he would have passed Finney's record much earlier. After injury forced his retirement he became assistant trainer at Burnden Park before joining Stockport County as assistant manager. He later rejoined the Wanderers as goalkeeping coach, but eventually left the game to become a representative for a chemical company.

The Wanderers' 1958 FA Cup-winning team. Back row, left to right: Bill Ridding (Manager), Ralph Gubbins, Roy Hartle, Derek Hennin, Eddie Hopkinson, John Higgins, Bryan Edwards, Tommy Banks, George Taylor and Bert Sproston (Trainers). Front row: Brian Birch, Dennis Stevens, Nat Lofthouse, Ray Parry, Doug Holden.

Freddie Hill turned down an offer from his home-town team Sheffield Wednesday in the hope of getting regular first team football with the Trotters. He made his League debut as a replacement for Dennis Stevens in a 1–1 home draw against Newcastle United in April 1958. When Nat Lofthouse retired, Stevens moved to centre-forward to accommodate Hill on a permanent basis at inside-left and he responded by netting his first hat-trick for the club in a 6–0 mauling of Chelsea. After only three seasons of League football he was chosen for the England Under-23 side and in October 1962 he played in his first full international against Northern Ireland in Belfast.

Hill's second hat-trick in Bolton colours came in a 3-2 win over Sheffield United in March 1963, the club's first home game for three months after one of the worst winters on record. He went on to score 79 goals in 412 games for the Wanderers before leaving Burnden Park in the summer of 1969 to join Halifax Town. He had almost signed for Liverpool during the height of his career but failed a medical owing to high blood pressure. He later played for Manchester City before ending his career with Peterborough United.

An England schoolboy and youth international, Warwick Rimmer was a nephew of the former Sheffield Wednesday player Ellis Rimmer and made his debut in the club's first Football League Cup tie at Hull City in October 1960. Strong in the tackle, the Merseyside-born defensive wing-half soon established himself in the Wanderers' side and was ever-present in three seasons. Though he twice suffered relegation with the Trotters, he captained the side that won the Third Division Championship in 1972/73 when his experience helped the young Paul Jones at the heart of the Bolton defence.

One of the club's most loyal servants, he played in 528 League and Cup games, scoring 17 goals for Bolton, but in March 1975 he left to join Crewe Alexandra. After making 128 League appearances for the Railwaymen he coached and managed the Gresty Road club before coaching in Sierra Leone. He returned to Bolton as the club's commercial manager before serving Tranmere Rovers in a similar capacity and later as their youth development officer.

After working his way through the junior ranks, Dave Hatton made his first team debut in a 1–1 draw at Leicester City in April 1962. The strong-tackling half-back then had a run at left-back in 1962/63 in place of the injured Syd Farrimond before establishing himself the following season. Hatton missed very few games over the next six seasons and had appeared in 259 League and Cup games when in September 1969 he joined Blackpool for a fee of £40,000.

He was badly missed by the Wanderers but helped the Seasiders win promotion to the First Division at the end of his first season with the Bloomfield Road club. After Blackpool were relegated Hatton continued to be a regular member of a side that was constantly pushing for promotion to the top flight. He had played in 274 games for the Seasiders before joining Bury as player-manager, but after the club narrowly avoided relegation to the Fourth Division in 1978/79 he was sacked.

Hindley-born left-back Syd Farrimond was an England Youth international who, after making his debut in a goalless draw against Preston North End at Deepdale in October 1958, understudied Tommy Banks before taking over on a regular basis in 1961/62 when he was ever-present. However, Farrimond didn't quite have the timing of the England international and his occasional vigorous tackling saw him sent off on a number of occasions.

He was a member of the Wanderers' side for the next ten seasons; he lost his place to Dave Hatton and Charlie Cooper but always won it back at their expense. Farrimond went on to appear in 404 League and Cup games for Bolton, his only goal for the club coming in a 1–1 home draw against Norwich City in March 1967. After eventually losing his place to the up-and-coming Don McAllister, he left Burnden Park on a free transfer following a dispute over a loyalty bonus. He joined Tranmere Rovers and appeared in 134 league games for the Prenton Park club before coaching spells with Halifax, Sunderland and Leeds United.

One of the most exciting players ever to play for the club, Francis Lee made his league debut for the Wanderers as a 16-year-old amateur in November 1960 after playing in only eight Central League games. Partnering the 35-year-old Nat Lofthouse, Lee scored a goal and got booked in a 3–1 win over Manchester City. He signed professional forms for the Wanderers in summer 1961 and after winning a regular first team place at the start of the 1962/63 season he topped Bolton's goal charts for five successive seasons. He netted the first of his two hat-tricks for the club in a 5–4 defeat at West Bromwich Albion in September 1962 with two of his goals coming from the penalty spot. Lee was one of the game's most deadly penalty-takers, scoring 26 of his 106 goals in that fashion. His second hat-trick came in a 3–1 win at Preston North End in February 1967 but later that year the goalscoring winger, who had put in a number of transfer requests, left Burnden Park to join Manchester City for £65,000.

At Maine Road he was one of the successes in a team that enjoyed one of the greatest eras in the club's history. He hit three hat-tricks for City including a spectacular threesome in the Manchester derby of 1970/71. In 1971/72 Lee topped the First Division goalscorers with 33 goals including 15 from the penalty spot – a record! For this achievement he was awarded the bronze boot in the Golden Boot competition. Lee was also a vital part of Sir Alf Ramsey's England squad and had gone to Mexico to defend the World Cup in 1970. Lee scored 10 goals in his 27 international appearances. After scoring 143 goals in 320 games for City he joined Derby County, where he helped the Rams win the League Championship. After securing millionaire status via his thriving paper business he became Manchester City chairman, relinquishing his position in 1998.

Wyn Davies had a spell with Llanberis before joining his home-town club Caernarfon. From there he entered League football with Wrexham and scored 26 goals in 67 first team games, including a hat-trick on his last appearance for the Robins as Hartlepool United were beaten 10–1. In March 1962 he joined the Wanderers in a transfer deal worth £20,000 in cash plus Ernie Phythian, who was reportedly valued at £10,000. He made his debut in a 5–1 defeat at Wolverhampton Wanderers and after that missed very few games in his four and a half seasons with the club.

After winning the first of 34 Welsh caps in 1964 'Wyn the Leap', as he was popularly known, scored his first hat-trick for the club in a 3–0 win over Southampton. He ended the 1964/65 season as the club's top scorer with 25 goals in 38 games. His performances for the Wanderers led to his name being linked with a number of top clubs and in October 1966 after scoring 74 goals in 170 games he joined Newcastle United for £80,000. He helped the Magpies win the Fairs Cup before winding down his career with the two Manchester clubs, Blackpool, Crystal Palace, Stockport County and Crewe Alexandra.

Now secretary of the Professional Footballers' Association, Gordon Taylor joined the Wanderers on amateur forms, turning professional in January 1962 after six months as an apprentice at Burnden Park. He made his league debut in a 4–0 defeat v. Wolverhampton Wanderers at Molineux in March 1963, though it was midway through the following season before he won a regular place in the side. Though he made his name on the left wing, Taylor was able to play on either flank. An ever-present in 1964/65 when the club finished third in Division Two, Taylor went on to score 46 goals in 286 games before joining Birmingham City for a fee of £18,000 in December 1970.

He helped the Blues win promotion from Division Two in 1971/72 and was a member of the side in two FA Cup semi-finals in 1972 and 1975. In March 1976, after having scored 10 goals in 203 games, he returned to the north-west to play for Blackburn Rovers. He spent just over two years at Ewood Park, a season with Vancouver Whitecaps in the NASL and then two full seasons with Bury before taking a job with the PFA on a full-time basis after serving on the committee during his playing days at Gigg Lane.

Farnworth-born Roy Greaves made his League debut in October 1965, aged 18, in a 1–0 defeat at Leyton Orient. The following Saturday he played at centre-forward for his first home game and scored both Bolton's goals in a 3–2 defeat by Southampton. He then settled into the Wanderers' side at inside-forward, becoming a regular in 1967/68 when he topped the club's goalscoring charts, as he did the following season. Despite these achievements, he failed to win over the home fans and was often subjected to mindless criticism. The turning point in his career came when manager Jimmy Armfield moved him into midfield after relegation to the Third Division in 1971.

When the Wanderers won the Third Division Championship in 1972/73 Greaves was ever-present and a cornerstone of the side that spent the next five seasons in Division Two before winning a place in the top flight. By then Roy Greaves had become captain and it was he who lifted the Second Division Championship trophy aloft at the end of the 1977/78 season. In his debut season in the First Division he missed only one game, but the following term a combination of injuries and advancing years cost him his place. He had scored 85 goals in 575 games when in March 1980 he left Bolton to play for the Seattle Sounders in the NASL. After his stint in America he returned to become player-coach at Rochdale, thus giving him the distinction of having played in every division of the League.

A training session at Bromwich Street which sees Francis Lee, Freddie Hill, Brian Bromley and Gordon Taylor under the watchful eyes of Nat Lofthouse (left) and George Taylor (fourth from left).

An instinctive goalscorer, John Byrom began his Football League career with his home-town club Blackburn Rovers where he scored 45 goals in 108 league games before Bill Ridding signed him for the Wanderers for a fee of £25,000 in summer 1966. Initially he had linked well with Wyn Davies and Francis Lee, but within a couple of months both had left Burnden Park. It was 1969/70 before 'JB' achieved the hoped-for prolific returns, for after netting hat-tricks in the first two games of the season he ended the campaign with 25 senior goals. The following season Bolton were relegated and as the club's most saleable asset he was made available for transfer. Fortunately he stayed to top the Wanderers' goalscoring charts in 1972/73 and win a Third Division Championship medal.

On the club's return to the Second Division he was again top scorer with 24 goals. In the FA Cup tie against Stoke City, he hit a hat-trick in Bolton's 3–2 win, popping up on his own goal line in the last minute to clear and then salute the fans! He had scored 130 goals in 351 games before being given a free transfer in 1976 and returning to Ewood Park for a brief Indian summer.

Liverpool-born John Ritson made his debut for the Wanderers in a 1–0 defeat at Queen's Park Rangers in October 1967, in the number seven shirt worn two weeks earlier by Francis Lee. However, it was at right-back that Ritson was to make a name for himself, appearing in 378 games in 11 seasons with the club. Though he only scored 13 goals for Bolton, he was renowned for unleashing virtually unstoppable blasts on goal and in 1977/78, his last season with the club, he scored vital goals in the club's 1–0 win at Mansfield Town and in the third round FA Cup replay against Spurs which Bolton won 2–1.

He won a Third Division Championship medal in 1972/73, but after helping the Wanderers win the Second Division title in 1977/78 failed to make an appearance in the top flight, being sold to neighbours Bury for a fee of £25,000. After making 41 League appearances for the Shakers he returned to Burnden Park as a non-contract player, but only played a handful of games in the club's Central League side.

Bolton-born winger Terry Wharton followed his father into the Football League and scored on his debut for Wolverhampton Wanderers in a 2–0 win over Ipswich Town in November 1961. He was the Molineux club's first-choice right-winger for the next five and a half seasons, netting his first hat-trick for the club in a 7–0 win over West Bromwich Albion. He helped Wolves win promotion to the First Division in 1966/67, scoring another hat-trick in a 7–1 home defeat of Cardiff City. He had scored 79 goals in 242 games for Wolves when he joined his home-town club for a fee of £70,000.

He made his Bolton debut in a 1–1 draw at Preston North End, replacing Francis Lee who had just joined Manchester City. Wharton became the club's penalty-taker and in 1969/70, when the Wanderers finished sixteenth in the Second Division, he missed just four games and scored 10 goals. He began the following season by scoring his first hat-trick for the club in a 4–2 home win over Luton Town, but after scoring 30 goals in 110 games he left to join Crystal Palace before ending his League career with a single appearance for Walsall.

Wembley-born Gareth Williams began his Football League career with Cardiff City after impressing in local schools football with future Welsh international Graham Moore. He gained a regular spot in the Bluebirds' midfield during the 1962/63 season and midway through the following campaign was made club captain. Over the next three seasons he was a virtual ever-present but in October 1967 after scoring 14 goals in 161 League games he joined Bolton for a fee of £45,000.

He made his debut for the Wanderers in a 2–0 home win over Norwich City and scored his first goal for the club five matches later as Charlton Athletic were beaten by a similar score. Despite becoming club captain, Williams had a poor disciplinary record and in November 1969 was suspended by the Wanderers for refusing to train with the rest of the team. He never recaptured the form of his Ninian Park days and in October 1971 after scoring 12 goals in 117 games he joined Bury for £5,000. He made 42 League appearances for the Gigg Lane club before leaving to join the prison service. He later managed a Fylde coast hotel before moving to live in Gran Canaria where he runs a bar.

After turning down offers from both Manchester City and United, Garry Jones joined the Wanderers as an apprentice before turning professional in January 1968. His first game in Bolton's colours was in a 3–0 defeat at Huddersfield Town in March 1969, although it was 1970/71 before he began to establish himself in the Wanderers' side.

On 5 October 1971 Jones hit the headlines when he scored a hat-trick in a 3–0 League Cup win over Manchester City. The following season he helped Bolton win the Third Division Championship when he netted 20 League and Cup goals, his best season in terms of goals scored. After this he suffered a series of niggling injuries and a loss of form, but after a loan spell with Sheffield United returned to be the club's joint top scorer in 1974/75 with 13 goals. Following the signing of Frank Worthington, Jones, who had scored 55 goals in 247 League and Cup games, joined Blackpool before ending his League career with Hereford United.

The best footballing centre-half to have played for the Wanderers since the Second World War, Paul Jones joined the club on leaving school in Ellesmere Port. After progressing through the club's junior ranks, he was one of a number of teenagers played against Sheffield United in January 1971, a match the Wanderers won 2–1. After replacing John Hulme at the start of the following season, Jones missed very few games over the next 12 seasons and was ever-present in 1972/73, 1974/75 and 1976/77. He won a Third Division Championship medal in 1973 and five years later a Second Division Championship medal, though he sustained an injury that restricted his appearances during that campaign.

During the club's stay in the First Division he had a spell at right-back but lacked the pace to fill the role on a regular basis. Following the club's relegation to the Third Division Jones, who had scored 43 goals in 506 games, left the Wanderers to play for Huddersfield Town. After that he was called up into the England squad during Don Revie's reign as manager, and had spells with Oldham Athletic and Blackpool before playing non-league football for a number of clubs.

After being rejected by Coventry City as a youngster, Don McAllister had better luck with his local club, Bolton Wanderers. The Radcliffe-born defender soon established himself in the club's Central League side and captained the club to victory in the Lancashire Youth Cup Final.

He made his first team debut in a goalless home draw against Norwich City in the final game of the 1969/70 season before winning a regular first team place midway through the following season. Although the Wanderers were relegated in his first season in the team, he helped Bolton win the Third Division title in 1972/73 when he missed just one game. Earning a reputation as one of the best defenders in the Second Division, he had appeared in 177 League and Cup games for Bolton when in February 1975 he joined Tottenham Hotspur for £80,000.

He helped the White Hart Lane club climb out of the Second Division in 1977/78 and re-establish themselves as a First Division force. But following a bad injury in 1980/81 McAllister, who had played in 202 games for Spurs, left to join Charlton Athletic where he played his last game in the 4–1 defeat of the Wanderers – the match that sent the club back to the Third Division.

A product of the club's youth side, Sam Allardyce made his league debut for the Wanderers against Notts County, the club he now manages, in November 1973. Following the departure of Don McAllister to Tottenham Hotspur, Allardyce won a regular place at the heart of the Bolton defence. During his time at Burnden Park Allardyce scored a number of spectacular goals, perhaps none more so than the fearsome header from fully 18 yards against Second Division promotion rivals Sunderland in December 1975.

Impressive in the air, he helped the club win the Second Division Championship in 1977/78, but after relegation two seasons later Allardyce left to join Sunderland for a fee of £150,000. After just one season at Roker Park he moved to Millwall, followed by brief spells at both Coventry and Huddersfield before he rejoined the Wanderers. Sadly he was hampered by injuries, and after appearing in 231 games in which he scored 24 goals he joined Preston North End. After helping the Lilywhites win promotion to the Third Division he became the club's youth coach, before breaking into management with Blackpool. He is now manager of Notts County whom he led to the Third Division Championship in 1997/98.

One of the club's greatest utility players, Peter Nicholson joined the Wanderers from Blackpool in the summer of 1971 after starting his career with Carlisle United. He played his first game for the club in a 2–2 draw at Oldham Athletic on the opening day of the 1971/72 season.

Though he made most of his appearances at right-back, he wore all the different numbered outfield shirts in 11 seasons at Burnden Park. He won a Third Division Championship medal in 1972/73 when he scored in each of the last three games of the season, and a Second Division Championship medal in 1977/78. There were those who thought he would struggle in the top flight but he held his own and went on to score 14 goals in 370 League and Cup games before leaving Burnden in May 1982 to join Rochdale. He later ended his career with Carlisle United before returning to Bolton where he helped out with commercial activities.

Glasgow-born goalkeeper Charlie Wright began his career with Rangers but, unable to break into the first team, he joined Workington. In 1960 he gained three international caps for Hong Kong while on National Service and in the match against Peru he saved a penalty. Later he was voted Hong Kong Player of the Year. When he returned to the UK, he played for Grimsby Town and Charlton Athletic before joining the Wanderers in June 1971.

After making his debut in a 2–2 draw at Oldham Athletic, he went on to be ever-present, helping Bolton register their best goals against record since 1925. Wright had a great sense of humour and continually chatted to spectators behind the goal. In 1972/73 he won a Third Division Championship medal with the Trotters but had to retire a year later through a persistent back injury after appearing in 109 games. After managing York City he took charge of the Wanderers but left the club in December 1985.

Tony Dunne joined Manchester United from League of Ireland club Shelbourne United for £3,500 in August 1960. He made 530 appearances for United, playing in the 1963 FA Cup-winning team, the Championship sides of 1964/65 and 1966/67 and in the 1968 European Cup Final when he gave one of the greatest displays of his career. Capped 32 times by the Republic of Ireland, he left Old Trafford in August 1973 and joined the Wanderers on a free transfer.

He made his debut in a 1–0 defeat at Bristol City on the opening day of the 1973/74 season. However, his form during that campaign was inconsistent and it was the following season before he showed his true capabilities. He was a regular member of the Bolton side in 1975/76 and 1976/77 when the Wanderers narrowly missed out on promotion to the top flight, and was still there in 1977/78 when they won the Second Division Championship. He won a further six caps for the Republic of Ireland while with Bolton but left the club after playing in 192 games. In 1980 he returned to Burnden Park, first as coach, then as assistant manager to Stan Anderson, leaving when he was replaced by George Mulhall in the spring of 1981.

Having appeared in the Wanderers' Central League side while still at school, Barry Siddall, the Ellesmere Port-born goalkeeper, went on to win England Youth honours before making his League debut for the Trotters in a 3–2 defeat at Walsall in October 1972. Following the retirement of Charlie Wright, Siddall made a great impact on the club's return to the Second Division and went on to appear in 133 consecutive League games. After appearing in 158 games for the Wanderers, Siddall joined Sunderland in September 1976 for £80,000.

He made his debut against Aston Villa and went on to appear in 103 consecutive League games immediately following his first appearance. He played in 189 League and Cup games for the Wearsiders and after a loan spell at Darlington joined Port Vale. Loan spells at Blackpool and Stoke City followed before he was transferred to the Potters for £20,000. He went on loan to Tranmere Rovers and Manchester City before signing for Blackpool in the summer of 1986 on a free transfer. He later played for Stockport County, Hartlepool United, Carlisle United, Chester City and Preston North End, eventually taking the total of League appearances for this much-travelled 'keeper to 613.

After beginning his Football League career with Preston North End, Peter Thompson joined Liverpool for £35,000 in August 1963. There were few more exciting sights in the Football League than to see Peter Thompson running at defenders with the ball at his feet. In nine seasons at Anfield he played in just over 400 games, scoring 54 goals. In his first season with the Reds he won four England Under-23 caps and also played his first full international. He was eventually capped 16 times by England while at Anfield, collecting League and FA Cup honours as well.

After losing his place to Steve Heighway he joined Bolton on loan in December 1973 and made his debut in a 1–0 home win over Sunderland. A month later he signed on a permanent basis, giving the Wanderers an exciting new attacking dimension. A great crowd favourite, he helped the club through one of its most exciting periods but at the end of the 1977/78 season after which he had played in 132 games, he left the game to run a hotel in the Lake District.

Neil Whatmore was still an apprentice when he made his debut for Bolton in April 1973, scoring twice in a victory at Swansea with Wanderers well on their way to the Third Division Championship.

He immediately became a regular in the Wanderers' team following their promotion to Division Two and in 1976/77 his 31 goals in League and Cup made him the third top scorer in the entire Football League. Six of his goals were scored in the League Cup, including the strike at Everton in a 1–1 draw in the first leg of the semi-final.

Whatmore was ever-present and top scored with 19 goals as Bolton won the Second Division in style in 1977/78. He moved into midfield for the club's return to the top flight but then top scored in each of the next two seasons before leaving to join Birmingham City for £340,000 in August 1981. The goals were slow in coming at St Andrew's and after a loan spell at Oxford he returned to Bolton in a similar capacity, and took his tally of goals to 121 in 338 games before joining Oxford on a permanent basis. After spells with Burnley and Mansfield, he rejoined Bolton again before becoming reserve team coach at Field Mill.

The Bolton side that won promotion to the top flight as Second Division champions in 1977/78. Back row, left to right: Garry Jones, Steve Taylor, Roy Greaves, John Ritson, Mike Walsh, Brian Smith. Middle row: Alan Waldron, Terry Poole, Neil Whatmore, Sam Allardyce, Jim McDonagh, Peter Nicholson. Front row: Tony Dunne, Ray Train, Andy Clement, Paul Jones, Peter Reid, Willie Morgan, Peter Thompson.

After two seasons of First Division football, the Wanderers were relegated in 1979/80. Back row, left to right: Paul Jones, Tadeus Nowak, Len Cantello, Mike Walsh, Sam Allardyce, Neil McNab. Middle row: Stan Anderson (Assistant Manager), Peter Nicholson, Jim McDonagh, Alan Gowling, Terry Poole, David Hoggan, Jim Hedridge (Physio), Ian Greaves (Manager). Front row: David Burke, Brian Smith, Roy Greaves, Neil Whatmore, Peter Reid, Dave Clement.

Peter Reid was a member of the successful Huyton Boys side that caused something of an upset when they won the English Schools Trophy in 1970. He had the chance to join a number of clubs as an apprentice but opted for the Wanderers and in October 1974 made his first team debut as a substitute in a home match against Orient. An ever-present for the next two seasons, Reid's cultured midfield play and his intense desire to be involved at all times were features of Bolton's Second Division championship-winning side of 1977/78. On New Year's Day 1979 he collided with Everton goalkeeper George Wood on a snow-covered Burnden Park and broke his leg. He eventually returned to the side on a weekly contract but broke his leg again in Bolton's match at Barnsley.

He had scored 25 goals in 261 games for the Wanderers when he joined Everton for £60,000 in December 1982. In 1984/85 he was voted the Players' Player of the Year as Everton came close to winning the treble of League, FA Cup and European Cup Winners' Cup. After spells as a player-coach, the England international later entered management with Manchester City and is now in charge of Sunderland.

Mancunian Mike Walsh joined Bolton straight from school, and after working his way up through the club's Youth and Central League teams made his Football League debut as a substitute in a 3–2 win at Nottingham Forest in February 1975. Though he started his career as a left-back, he was able to play both at centre-half and in midfield, though the next two seasons following his debut were still spent deputising for first team regulars. Following an injury to Paul Jones, Walsh started Bolton's Second Division Championship-winning season of 1977/78 alongside Sam Allardyce and missed just one game as the Trotters finished two points ahead of runners-up Tottenham Hotspur.

During Bolton's two seasons back in the top flight, Walsh was an ever-present, playing in 126 consecutive League games before injury ended the run. Despite the Wanderers' defence coming under a lot of pressure, Walsh was in commanding form and it came as no surprise when he moved to Everton for £90,000 with Jim McDonagh returning to Burnden Park in the deal. Capped five times by the Republic of Ireland, he had loan spells with Norwich and Burnley before joining Manchester City; he later played for Blackpool. In December 1990 he entered football management with Bury.

Goalkeeper Jim McDonagh joined the Wanderers from his home-town club, Rotherham United, in August 1976, initially on loan. His first game for the club was in a 3–0 home defeat by Blackpool, and after Barry Siddall's transfer to Sunderland he kept his place in the side for the remainder of that season. He was an ever-present for the next three seasons and in 1977/78 helped the club win promotion to the First Division when he only let in 33 goals, the fewest ever conceded by the Wanderers in a 42-match programme. He holds the club record for the most consecutive League appearances, having played in 161 games from his debut.

Following Bolton's relegation in 1980, he joined Everton for a fee of £250,000 and it was while with the Goodison Park club that he won the first of 24 full caps for the Republic of Ireland. Within a year he had returned to Burnden Park in the deal that saw Mike Walsh join the Blues. McDonagh, who scored from a long kick in the 3–0 win over Burnley in January 1983, played in 274 games before joining Notts County. He later played for Birmingham City, Gillingham, Sunderland, Scarborough, Huddersfield Town and Charlton Athletic.

One of the best wingers in British football since the war, Willie Morgan began his career with Burnley and made his League debut in a 1–0 win over Sheffield Wednesday in April 1963. He won a regular place on the Clarets' right wing and quickly developed into one of the most feared wingers in the game. Not surprisingly, his performances attracted the big city clubs, and after making his international debut for Scotland against Northern Ireland in October 1967 he joined Manchester United for £117,000.

He soon settled in at Old Trafford alongside Best, Law and Charlton, and in March 1969 netted a hat-trick in a 6–1 win over Queen's Park Rangers. After United had lost their First Division status Morgan helped them win promotion in 1974/75 before returning to Burnley. However, the move was not a success and he was soon on his way to Bolton.

He was instrumental in Wanderers' success in the Second Division over the next few seasons, fourth in both 1976 and 1977 and the Championship in 1978 when he missed just one game. While at Burnden Park he was able to enjoy summer loan periods in the NASL. After scoring 12 goals in 179 games he moved to Blackpool where he ended his League career.

David Burke made his debut for the Wanderers as a replacement for the injured Tony Dunne in a League Cup second round tie against Chelsea in August 1978. When Bolton entertained the Stamford Bridge club in the First Division later that season, Burke scored his only goal for the club in another 2–1 win. Following Tony Dunne's retirement the England Youth international established himself as the club's first-choice left-back, though he was also able to play on the left side of midfield. However, after three seasons with the club in which he had appeared in 76 games, he left to play for Huddersfield Town.

He made 189 League appearances for the Terriers, helping them win promotion to the Second Division in 1982/83. In October 1987 he joined Crystal Palace for a fee of £78,000 and was captain when they won promotion to the top flight via the play-offs in 1989. He returned to Burnden in summer 1990, and though at first he found it difficult to displace Barry Cowdrill he went on to take his total of first team outings in his two spells with the club to 214 before leaving to join Blackpool, where he ended his League career.

Wednesbury-born John Thomas was a carpenter by trade and in August 1977 he joined Everton. Unable to break into the first team at Goodison Park, he had loan spells with Tranmere Rovers and Halifax Town before joining the Wanderers on a free transfer. He made his debut as a substitute in a 3–1 home win over Leyton Orient in December 1980. In 1981/82 he suffered a number of injuries and only appeared in five games. However, his only goal of that campaign was the club's 5000th goal against Grimsby Town, a match the Wanderers lost 2–1.

In May 1982 he joined Chester City and in his only season with the club top scored with 22 goals. He then joined Lincoln City and netted 21 goals in 71 games before signing for Preston North End for £15,000. He was a great favourite at Deepdale and his 27 goals in 1986/87 helped the Lilywhites win promotion. He joined Bolton for a second time in the summer of 1987 and top scored the following season with 28 goals, including hat-tricks against Peterborough United and Newport County, as Bolton won promotion to the Third Division. He had scored 44 goals in 110 games when he joined West Bromwich, later playing for Preston, Hartlepool and Halifax.

On 21 April 1979 Frank Worthington scored what was quite rightly described as the Goal of the Season. Worthy flicked the ball over his own head before volleying it into the Ipswich Town net. The goal caught the Portman Road defenders completely unawares and was enjoyed not only by Bolton fans but by countless TV viewers on the day. It was the only game of the season that I missed, having had to take my mother to hospital after she had fallen and broken her arm!

Opposite: Frank Worthington was a talented footballer and an extrovert character who became a footballing hero at Burnden Park in what was a relatively short career there. He began his career with Huddersfield Town and after helping them to win the Second Division title in 1970 the chance came for him to join Liverpool. A fee of £150,000 had been agreed but a medical examination revealed that he had high blood pressure; Leicester City seized their chance and a cut-price Worthington moved to Filbert Street for £80,000. His elegant, effective centre-forward play was rewarded with an England call-up and he went on to make eight appearances at full international level – it should have been many more. He had scored 72 goals in 210 games for the Foxes when he joined Bolton on loan as Ian Greaves was searching for that extra quality to lift the Wanderers into the First Division after two near misses.

He scored on his debut against Stoke City and was signed permanently for £90,000. He soon rediscovered the style which had made him one of the best strikers in the game and in 1977/78 he helped the Wanderers win the Second Division Championship. The following season he proved his class as a target man and a finisher. Although Bolton struggled against relegation, Worthington ended the season with 24 League goals to top the First Division goalscoring charts. His televised goal against Ipswich Town won the Goal of the Season competition. He had scored 38 goals in 93 games when he moved on to Birmingham City for £150,000. He later had spells with Leeds United, Sunderland, Southampton, Brighton, Tranmere, Preston and Stockport County. One of the game's most gifted and colourful strikers, he made 757 league appearances in a career that saw him approaching his fortieth birthday before he left the first-class game.

London-born Jeff Chandler began his league career with Blackpool and scored on his debut in a 2–1 win at Blackburn Rovers in September 1977. He had scored seven goals in 37 League games when Leeds United paid £100,000 to take him to Elland Road in September 1979. Despite winning two caps for the Republic of Ireland, Chandler failed to settle at the Yorkshire club and in October 1981 he crossed the Pennines and joined the Wanderers for £40,000.

He made his debut in a 3–0 home win over Leicester City and over the next four seasons missed very few games, being an ever-present in 1983/84. That season saw him score 17 goals and that, coupled with the 20 he netted in 1984/85, prompted Derby County to sign him for £38,000, the fee being fixed by a tribunal. He helped the Rams win promotion from the Third Division in 1985/86 before, following a short loan spell with Mansfield Town, he rejoined the Wanderers. Yet in only his fourth game back he damaged ligaments, which forced him to miss most of that promotion-winning season. He had scored 48 goals including one in the Sherpa Van Trophy Final in 211 games when he left to join Cardiff City.

After playing both cricket and rugby at county level, Warren Joyce chose football as his preferred sport, joining Bolton as a junior before signing professional forms in 1982. The son of Walter Joyce who played for Burnley, Blackburn Rovers and Oldham Athletic, he made his debut as a substitute in a 5–0 defeat at Carlisle United in April 1983. He established himself as a Third Division regular in 1983/84 and was a virtual ever-present until injury kept him out of the Wanderers' side in early 1986, forcing him to miss the Freight Rover Trophy Final against Bristol City. After the Wanderers' relegation to the Fourth Division in 1987 Joyce, who had scored 21 goals in 221 games, joined Preston North End for £35,000.

He helped the Deepdale club to the play-offs in 1989 but after scoring 44 goals in 210 games left to sign for Plymouth Argyle for £160,000. But after only a year at Home Park he returned to the north-west to join Burnley. The tenacious midfielder made 90 appearances for the Clarets before signing for Hull City where his whole-hearted performances led to him sweeping the board with the club's Player of the Year awards.

The dynamic midfielder Steve Thompson impressed in a strong Bolton Youth side before making his first team debut in a goalless draw at Derby County in November 1982. But it wasn't until the following season that he began to make his mark and over the next eight campaigns he was a virtual ever-present. He appeared for the Wanderers in the Freight Rover Trophy Final at Wembley in 1986 when they lost 3–0 to Bristol City but was successful on his second visit to the Twin Towers in 1989 when Bolton beat Torquay United 4–1 to lift the Sherpa Van Trophy. His performances helped the Wanderers reach the play-offs in seasons 1989/90 and 1990/91 but after scoring 57 goals in 422 games he left the club to join Luton Town in a £220,000 deal.

After less than two months at Kenilworth Road he was on the move again, this time to Leicester City. He helped the Filbert Street club to the First Division play-offs in seasons 1991/92 and 1992/93 and then again the following season when he made a substitute appearance as they eventually won a place in the top flight. Leaving Leicester in 1995 he returned to the north-west with Burnley, but is now playing with Rotherham United.

An electrician by trade, Tony Caldwell had played in local football with Irlam Town and was scoring prolifically for Horwich RMI when Bolton signed him for a bargain £2,000 in 1983. After impressing on a pre-season tour to Ireland the Salford-born striker was given his League debut in the opening game of the 1983/84 season against Wimbledon, which the Wanderers won 2–0. He scored in a victory at Bradford City the following week but really hit the headlines in the club's next home game when he scored five goals in an 8–1 victory over Walsall at Burnden Park to equal James Cassidy's club record that had stood for 93 years.

Caldwell ended the season as the club's top scorer with 23 goals in 38 games, a feat he was to achieve in each of his four seasons with the club. He had scored 78 goals in 176 games including a hat-trick in a 7–2 win over Plymouth Argyle in September 1984 when he left Bolton to join Bristol City for £27,500 – a fee decided by a tribunal transfer. But at Ashton Gate as with subsequent clubs Chester City, Grimsby Town and Stockport County, he failed to find his goalscoring touch.

After working his way through the club's junior teams and reserves, Jimmy Phillips made his first team debut as a substitute in a 1–0 defeat at home to Gillingham in April 1984.

Following Ray Deakin's departure to Burnley, Phillips established himself as the club's first choice left-back and appeared at Wembley when the Whites were beaten 3–0 by Bristol City in the Freight Rover Trophy Final of 1986.

However, in March 1987 Glasgow Rangers paid £75,000 to take the young Phillips to Ibrox Park and the following season he played in four European Cup ties for the Scottish champions. In the summer of 1988 he joined Oxford United for £110,000 before signing for Middlesbrough who were then managed by the current Wanderers' boss Colin Todd. While with 'Boro he helped them win promotion to the top flight as runners-up to Ipswich Town, but in the summer of 1993 he rejoined his home-town club for a fee of £300,000. He was ever-present in 1994/95 when the club won promotion to the Premiership and reached the League Cup Final. He won a First Division Championship medal in 1996/97 and has now taken his total of first team appearances in his two spells at the club to almost 400.

Central defender Mark Came joined the Wanderers from non-league Winsford United in April 1984 and made his first team debut five months later as a substitute in a 2–0 defeat at Doncaster Rovers. Over the next four seasons Came missed very few games, and in 1987/88 when the club won promotion he was rated one of the best defenders in the Fourth Division. The following season he was appointed the club's captain, but after leading the Wanderers to victory in the Lancashire Cup he broke a leg in a League Cup tie at Chester and missed the rest of the season.

Despite regaining full fitness, he found it difficult to displace Winstanley and Crombie at the heart of the Bolton defence, and though he stayed at Burnden Park until December 1992 his role tended to be that of understudy. He had scored 11 goals in 259 games when he joined Chester City for £10,000 and in 1993/94 helped them to runners-up spot in the Fourth Division. After appearing in 47 games for Chester he left on a free transfer to play for Exeter City. He played in 70 games for the Grecians before returning to Winsford United as player-coach.

Appearing in every outfield position, Bolton-born utility player Julian Darby made the first of his 345 appearances for the club at full-back in a 3–1 home defeat by Blackpool in March 1986.

In nine seasons with the club, Darby scored 52 goals, none more vital than his 27th minute equaliser against Torquay United in the Sherpa Van Trophy Final at Wembley in 1989.

After establishing himself as a first team regular in 1986/87 he missed very few games and in 1989-90 when the Wanderers reached the play-offs he was ever-present. Sadly during the 1991/92 season Darby was made the scapegoat by a section of the Bolton crowd for the overall failure of the Burnden side. After that his appearances were limited and in October 1993 he joined his former manager Phil Neal at Coventry City for a fee of £150,000.

He left Highfield Road in November 1995 to join West Bromwich Albion for £250,000 but in the summer of 1997, after playing in 44 games for the Baggies, he returned to Lancashire, signing for Preston North End in a player exchange deal.

Goalkeeper Dave Felgate graduated through the youth system at Burnden Park but was unable to break into the first team and was loaned out to gain experience with both Rochdale and Crewe Alexandra. In September 1980 he joined Lincoln City for a fee of £25,000 and while at Sincil Bank won his only full cap for Wales against Romania at the Racecourse Ground in 1984.

After appearing in 198 League games for the Imps he had a short loan spell with Cardiff City before signing for Grimsby Town in summer 1985. However, in February 1986 he returned to Burnden Park on loan and kept a clean sheet on his debut in a 4–0 win over Newport County. After helping the club reach the Freight Rover Trophy Final he rejoined Grimsby before signing for the Wanderers on a permanent basis.

Despite suffering relegation to the Fourth Division in his first season in the team, he helped them win promotion and the Sherpa Van Trophy in 1989. Missing very few games while with the Wanderers, he had made 300 appearances when he joined Chester. Felgate later played for Wigan Athletic and now keeps goal for Leigh RMI for whom he was outstanding in the FA Cup games against Fulham in 1998/99.

Defender Mark Winstanley was offered a YTS place at Burnden and after graduating through the club's youth ranks was still a trainee when he made his debut in a 2–1 defeat at Bournemouth in March 1986.

Following two seasons on the fringe of first team action, he claimed a regular place in the Bolton defence in 1988/89 and scored three goals in the club's run-up to the Sherpa Van Trophy Final. The most crucial of these was his last-gasp equaliser in the second round tie against Wrexham which took the tie into extra time, when he then headed home a second.

The Wanderers reached the Third Division play-offs in 1990 where they were beaten by Notts County and though they went one better in the play-off finals of 1991, injury cost 'Beef' his place in the side. He was a regular in the Wanderers' side that achieved promotion from the new Second Division in 1992/93 as runners-up to Stoke and was prominent in the club's run to the fifth round of the FA Cup. However, he was not an automatic choice in 1993/94 and at the end of that season in which he took his total of appearances for Bolton to 285, he joined Burnley for £150,000.

Phil Brown began his League career with Hartlepool United, and after making his debut against Peterborough United in March 1980 went on to appear in 217 games before joining Halifax Town in summer 1985. Appointed the Shaymen's captain, he was the club's leading scorer in 1986/87 with 14 goals, one of which came against Bolton when he earned the Yorkshire side a second replay in the first round of the FA Cup.

The Wanderers paid £17,500 for Brown's services in June 1988, and after making his debut in a 2–0 defeat at Southend United on the opening day of the 1988/89 season he appeared in 171 consecutive League games before injury ruled him out of the Bournemouth game in April 1991. The Bolton manager at the time of Brown's arrival at Burnden Park was Phil Neal and he had no hesitation in handing him the captain's armband. At the end of his first season with the club he led them to success in the Sherpa Van Trophy and later through two disappointments in the Third Division promotion play-offs. Brown scored 17 goals in 332 games for the Wanderers before joining Blackpool as player-coach. He is now back with Bolton as coach.

A former England schoolboy international, Tony Philliskirk began his League career with Sheffield United and in 1983/84, his first season with the club, his eight goals helped the Blades win promotion to the Second Division. He had scored 20 goals in 80 games for the Yorkshire club before signing for Oldham Athletic. His stay at Boundary Park was short and in February 1989 he joined Preston North End – but after just four months at Deepdale he moved to Bolton for £50,000.

He made his debut in a 2–0 win at Cardiff City on the opening day of the 1989/90 season, scoring the Wanderers' opening goal after just four minutes. He ended the season as the club's leading scorer with 25 goals and did so again in 1990/91 when two of his 28 strikes helped Bolton beat Bury in the play-off semi-finals. The club's regular penalty-taker, he continued to score goals with great regularity but, after losing his place to John McGinlay, the Sunderland-born striker who had scored 75 goals in 182 games, joined Peterborough United for £80,000. He later returned to the north-west to play for Burnley and scored against the Wanderers in a 1–1 draw. In December 1995 he joined Cardiff City, later taking refereeing examinations.

David Reeves joined Sheffield Wednesday in summer 1986 but made his League debut while on loan with Scunthorpe United, scoring twice in a 3–1 win over Exeter City. In October 1987 he returned to the Irons for a second loan spell and in his first game netted a hat-trick in a 3–2 defeat of Hereford United. The following month he joined Burnley on loan and in his first game scored for the Clarets in a 2–1 win over the Wanderers! He eventually made his league debut for the Owls but after 17 games he was signed by Bolton for a tribunal-set fee of £80,000.

His only hat-trick for the Wanderers came in a 4–1 Autoglass Trophy win over Rochdale in December 1991. Reeves missed very few games in his first three seasons with the club, but his opportunities for first team football were restricted following the signing of Andy Walker. Forming a prolific goalscoring partnership with Tony Philliskirk, he had scored 42 goals in 173 games before leaving Bolton to join Notts County. Later he played for Carlisle United and helped the Brunton Park club win the Third Division Championship. After a brief spell with Preston North End he joined Second Division Chesterfield.

Darwen-born midfielder Mark Patterson began his career as a left-winger with his local club Blackburn Rovers. He went on to score 20 goals (including a hat-trick in a 6–1 win over Sheffield United) in 101 league games for the Ewood Park club before joining Preston North End in the summer of 1988. He helped the Lilywhites to the Third Division play-off, but in February 1990 Bury paid £80,000 to take him to Gigg Lane. After helping the Shakers reach that season's play-offs where they lost to Tranmere Rovers, he left Bury midway through the following campaign, signing for Bolton for a fee of £65,000.

He made his debut as a substitute in a 1–1 draw at Bradford City, and though injury kept him out of that season's play-offs he missed very few games over the following five seasons. When the Wanderers were promoted from the new Second Division in 1992/93 Patterson's presence on the left of midfield was an important factor in the club's success. He scored a number of vital goals, including the FA Cup third round equaliser against Everton in January 1994, but in December 1995 after scoring 14 goals in 215 games he joined Sheffield United for £150,000.

A boyhood Everton fan, Alan Stubbs graduated through Bolton's youth ranks before making his League debut as a substitute in a 1–0 home defeat by Bradford City. Three days later he scored on his full debut in a 2–1 League Cup win over Huddersfield Town. He seemed to spend most of that season on the bench although he did play at Wembley in the play-off final against Tranmere Rovers. Able to play in a number of positions, he made rapid strides over the next couple of seasons, establishing himself at the heart of the Bolton defence. Always dangerous when in the opposing penalty area, he scored vital goals against Everton and Aston Villa in the club's run to the FA Cup quarter-finals in 1993/94.

After that he won international recognition when he was awarded a 'B' cap for England against Northern Ireland at Hillsborough. He captained the Wanderers to play-off success against Reading and though he missed part of the club's campaign in the Premiership he returned to play his part in the club's fight against relegation. He had appeared in 256 games for Bolton when he left to join Celtic for £3.5 million but was sent off in his first League game for the Parkhead club.

Probably the best known of all the Wanderers' fans is Dave Higson. His 'ding-dong-do' commentaries on the club's videos have made him a cult figure, appearing on TV shows such as *Oddballs* and *Fantasy Football*. A lifelong fan, he is a familiar face at all Bolton games, home and away. The fans gave Dave a cake on his birthday on 5 November 1994 as Bolton left The Valley after beating Charlton Athletic 2–1.

Bolton fans gave Dave Higson this trophy before the FA Cup game against Arsenal in January 1994 as a thank you for all his entertaining commentaries. He was first asked to do commentaries for the videos in 1986 when his 'potential' was spotted while working in his spare time as a steward on one of the club's match coaches. He developed a good rapport with the players and management, and knew that if he ribbed them in his reports, they would good-naturedly get their own back.

All true Bolton fans will have seen the videos and surely will have smiled at Dave's stock phrases – 'Oh, I do believe he's given a penalty', 'Julian Darby, Jules as they call him here at Burnden Park', and of course the classic 'Mark Winstanley! Goal! Mark Winstanley! Winnie, Winnie, Winnie!'

KENNETH WOLSTENHOLME D.F.C.

August 7,
1995.

Mr. Dave Higson,
26 Chillam Street,
Morris Green,
Bolton.
<u>LANCASHIRE.</u>

Dear Dave,

I was saddened but not surprised when I read that you and Road Runner were no longer going to be involved with the videoing of the Wanderers' games in the coming season. One of the horrors of getting into The Premiership is that Sky TV, which provides millions of pounds to the clubs, has to be obeyed. They want videos of every Premiership game and insist on choosing who does the production. Naturally, it follows that whoever covers the games for Sky will want to produce the club video

Those videos will not be the commercial success as before because whereas you commentated as a confirmed Bolton fan, which the video buyers wanted, the future commentaries will be aimed at a much wider audience.

I would like you to know that the videos I saw of last season were excellent and as a Bolton fan I thought your enthusiasm and unashamed leaning towards the Bolton cause made the videos what they were. I was particularly thrilled by the second leg of the Swindon Coca-Cola cup match...even though I knew the result!

You did a great job and it was a pleasure to meet you and talk with you at the Burnley game. Good luck in the future.

Yours Sincerely,

Kenneth

Letter from Bolton-born commentator Kenneth 'They think it's all over – it is now' Wolstenholme to Dave 'Ding-Dong-Do' Higson, who deemed it an honour that the great man should take time out to write to him.

Liverpool fan Tony Kelly started his apprenticeship at Anfield in September 1982; however, after failing to make the grade he joined Derby County. After leaving the Baseball Ground he signed for Prescot Cables before Harry McNally gave him his chance in League football with Wigan Athletic. After moving to a midfield position he became a regular in the Latics side and played in 127 League and Cup games, scoring 22 goals including one in the club's Freight Rover Trophy win at Wembley.

He joined Stoke City for £80,000, but after just 45 games for the Potters moved to West Bromwich Albion. There followed loan spells at Chester and Colchester before Ian McNeill took him to Shrewsbury. He became captain at Gay Meadow and played in 120 games before joining the Wanderers in summer 1991. He made his debut in a 1–1 draw at home to Huddersfield Town and scored his first goals for the club on his return to Shrewsbury where the Wanderers won 3–1. He reached a creative peak during the club's FA Cup run of 1993/94 when he was on song; he gave the team a different dimension.

Affectionately known as 'Zico', Tony Kelly went on to score eight goals in 142 League and Cup games before joining Port Vale.

Goalkeeper Keith Branagan began his League career with Cambridge United and had made 134 first team appearances when Millwall paid £100,000 for his services in March 1988. Initially he was unable to break into the Lions' side but after a loan spell at Brentford he established himself in the Millwall side. He had helped the London club to the play-offs when injury struck and though he regained full fitness following a further loan spell, this time with Gillingham, he found it difficult to regain his place.

Wanderers' manager Bruce Rioch brought Branagan to Burnden Park on a free transfer and he made his debut in a 2–0 home win over Huddersfield Town on the opening day of the 1992/93 season. He was ever-present that season as the Wanderers won promotion from the Second Division but missed a good deal of the following campaign because of injury. The following season he was instrumental in the Wanderers reaching the League Cup Final and play-offs where he turned the game against Reading after saving a penalty. Since then the Republic of Ireland international 'keeper has been the Wanderers' first choice, and had played in 245 games until injury cost him his place.

The club's first fanzine *Wanderers Worldwide*, which cost 30 pence, started when a group of fans got together to produce an information service for all exiled Bolton fans.

Costing £1, one of the present fanzines, *White Love*, on sale during the 1998/99 season.

Winger David Lee began his career with Bury whom he helped to two Division Three play-offs, losing the second of them to the Wanderers. He appeared in 249 first team games for the Shakers, scoring 40 goals before moving into the top flight with Southampton who paid £350,000 for his services in summer 1991. Unable to settle on the south coast, he returned to the north-west in November 1992 when he joined Bolton on loan. His first match for the Wanderers was in a 3–1 win at Exeter City, and after impressing in all of his loan games he joined the club on a permanent basis for a fee of £300,000.

He played in every game for the rest of that season as the club won promotion to the Second Division as runners-up to Stoke City. He continued to torment the opposition defences in 1993/94 and ran Nigel Winterburn ragged in the FA Cup replay at Highbury when Bolton beat the Gunners 3–1. Lee's goals were quite often spectacular, probably the best being his solo effort against Norwich City in the 1994/95 League Cup. A broken ankle and a loss of confidence then limited his opportunities and after 199 appearances for the Wanderers he joined Wigan Athletic.

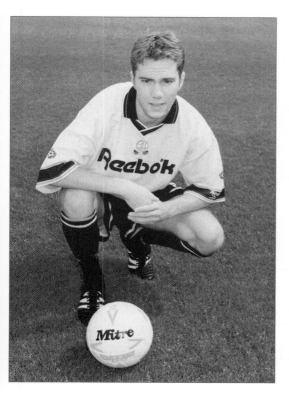

Republic of Ireland international Jason McAteer joined the Wanderers from Marine and made his League debut in November 1992 when he came on as a substitute for Scott Green in a 4–0 win over Burnley. His full first team debut came the following week in another 4–0 victory, this time against Rochdale in a second round FA Cup tie in which he scored a goal. After that he became a regular in the club's midfield and in 1993/94 he appeared in every League game and scored in both FA Cup matches against Arsenal, his performances earning him an international debut against Holland. In 1994/95 he was instrumental in the Wanderers reaching the League Cup Final against Liverpool and winning promotion to the Premiership via the play-offs.

Sadly the Birkenhead-born midfielder appeared in only four Premier League games for the Wanderers to take his total appearances for the club to 145 before he left Burnden Park to join Liverpool for £4.5 million – a new club record fee for an outgoing transfer. The nephew of former British and Empire middleweight boxing champion, Pat McAteer, he had appeared in more than 100 games for the Reds before joining Blackburn Rovers.

Football supporters don't come much bigger than Bolton's nationwide favourite, Lofty the Lion. A bulky 6ft 6in, he wears kit, extra, extra large and his size 26 feet are encased in studded boots specially made by Reebok!

Opposite: John McGinlay played his early football with Nairn County before spending a season in New Zealand playing for Hanimex. On his return he was signed by Gola League club Yeovil Town, and after spending three and a half seasons with the Somerset club joined Elgin City. His goalscoring achievements led to Shrewsbury manager Ian McNeill paying £25,000 for his services in February 1989. The following season he scored in both games against the Wanderers but in the summer of 1990 after he had scored 31 goals in 68 games for Shrewsbury he joined Bury for a fee of £175,000. While with the Shakers McGinlay hit a hat-trick against the Wanderers at a rain-soaked Burnden Park in a 3–1 win for the Gigg Lane club, but in January 1981 Bruce Rioch paid £80,000 to take him to Millwall. The London club reached the play-offs that season but in September 1992 Rioch, who was by now the Bolton boss, paid £125,000 to bring him to Burnden Park. He made his debut in a 1–0 defeat at Leyton Orient but ended his first season with 22 goals as the Wanderers won promotion and reached the fifth round of the FA Cup. His goals in both matches against Liverpool and the penalty-kick that beat Preston in the final game of the season endeared him to the hearts of Bolton fans.

In 1993/94 he netted 33 goals to equal the post-war club record held by Nat Lofthouse and Andy Walker for total goals in a season. His record included hat-tricks against Charlton Athletic and Middlesbrough. In 1994 he won the first of 13 Scottish caps when he scored in a 2–1 win over Austria. McGinlay, who netted another hat-trick in the 6–1 League Cup win over Spurs, went on to score 118 goals in 245 games, including the last goal at Burnden Park before joining Bradford City for £625,000 in November 1997.

Owen Coyle challenges for the ball in
Wanderers' 1–1 draw in the Anglo-Italian Cup
match in Pisa, where Jimmy Phillips scored
Bolton's goal.

Alan Thompson knocks the ball past the outstretched leg of his Ascoli opponent in Wanderers' Anglo-
Italian Cup match. Bolton drew 1–1, with Mark Seagraves netting for the Whites.

One of the game's most lethal finishers, Andy Walker began his career with Motherwell before joining Celtic. During the 1987/88 season Walker scored 31 goals as the 'Bhoys' won the League and Cup double – and he won the first of three full caps for Scotland.

After failing to fit in with the plans of new Celtic boss, Liam Brady, Walker had a loan stint at Newcastle United before joining Bolton in January 1992 on a similar basis. He made his debut as a substitute in a 2–2 draw at Exeter City, scoring with his first touch within minutes of coming on. The following month he joined the Wanderers on a permanent basis for £160,000, after which he could do no wrong. He scored 15 goals in 24 league games, and after netting after just 47 seconds in the opening game of the 1992/93 season he went on to score 26 league goals as the Wanderers won promotion to the First Division. His total of 33 goals equalled a post-war club record set by Nat Lofthouse twice during the 1950s. Sadly his season came to an end when he damaged his cruciate ligament in the match against Swansea City. He recovered to take his tally of goals to 55 in 87 games before rejoining Celtic for £550,000.

Alan Thompson began his career with Newcastle United but it was almost nipped in the bud when he broke his neck in a car crash, an injury which sidelined him for nearly 12 months before he courageously recovered. He appeared in 20 first team games for the Magpies before joining Bolton for £250,000 in the summer of 1993.

He made his debut in a goalless draw at Grimsby Town in August 1993 and scored his first goal for the club in the televised 4–3 victory over Nottingham Forest a month later. Thompson scored a number of memorable goals the following season, none more so than the strike in the Coca Cola Cup Final against Liverpool at Wembley. On the opening day of the 1995/96 season Thompson scored the Wanderers' first Premier League goal in a 3–2 defeat at Wimbledon, though it was to be his only League goal of a campaign in which he suffered a loss of form. He also scored the first goal at the Reebok Stadium, netting a penalty for Bolton against Spurs in September 1997. He had scored 42 goals in 198 games when his all-action displays prompted Aston Villa to pay £4.5 million for his services in June 1998.

Danish international Per Frandsen joined the Wanderers from FC Copenhagen in a double deal with Michael Johansen in the summer of 1996. An energetic and powerful midfielder, Frandsen made his league debut in a 1–1 draw at Port Vale on the opening day of the 1996/97 season and then scored the only goal of the game on his home debut three days later as the Wanderers beat Manchester City. His displays during the club's Division One Championship-winning season made him one of the campaign's best buys and in 1997/98 he was voted the players' Player of the Year after proving himself very much at home in the Premiership. His powerful long-range shooting brought him goals in the late-season wins over Leicester City and Sheffield Wednesday and his form, despite the Wanderers' relegation, led to him making two appearances for Denmark in the 1998 World Cup Finals in France.

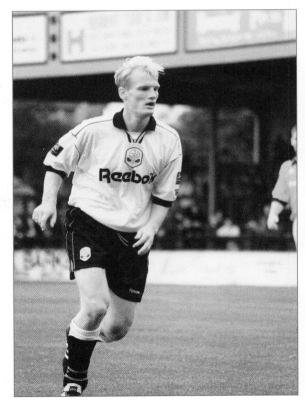

Nathan Blake began his career with Newport County before being taken on as a trainee by Chelsea. Unable to break into the first team at Stamford Bridge, he returned to South Wales and began his League career with his home-town club, Cardiff City. He soon established himself in the Bluebirds' side and in 1992/93 helped them win the Third Division Championship. He had scored 40 goals in 164 games when Sheffield United paid £300,000 to take him to Bramall Lane.

In his first full seasons with the Blades he top scored with 17 goals in 35 games and led the way again in 1994/95 with 12 goals in 22 games before Bolton paid £1.35 million for his services in December 1995. He made his debut in a 2–2 draw at Tottenham Hotspur but only managed one goal for the club during that 1995/96 season. He came into his own the following season, forming a prolific goalscoring partnership with John McGinlay and netting 24 League and Cup goals as the Wanderers returned to the top flight. Despite the club being relegated for a second time in three years, the Welsh international was Wanderers' top scorer, but after having scored 47 goals in 127 games he left the Reebok Stadium to join Premier League Blackburn Rovers for £4.25 million.

Along with his twin brother David, Dean Holdsworth joined Watford as an associated schoolboy in the summer of 1984, and after progressing to the Hornets' professional ranks made his League debut against Luton Town in December 1987. There followed loan spells at Carlisle United, Port Vale, Swansea and Brentford before he joined the Bees on a permanent basis in September 1989. He was an immediate success at Griffin Park and after helping the club win the Third Division Championship in 1991/92 Holdsworth, who had scored 75 goals in 137 games, joined Wimbledon for £750,000.

Despite a series of injuries including a hernia operation, he was the third top scorer in the Premier League with 19 goals. He was Wimbledon's leading scorer for the next four seasons, but in October 1997 after netting 76 goals in 208 games he became the Wanderers' most expensive signing when he joined the club for £3.5 million.

Though Wanderers' fans expected great things from him, a series of niggling injuries made life difficult for him. He scored the winner in his third match against Chelsea but ended the campaign with just three goals in 20 League games. In 1998/99 he was in much better form and scored a number of vital goals.

Gudni Bergsson was a law student at Reykjavik University when he was invited to join Spurs on trial. He was playing as an amateur for his local club, whom he helped win the Icelandic title in 1987 and the Icelandic Cup in 1988. With Spurs he appeared in 71 League games before joining the Wanderers for a fee of £115,000 in March 1995.

Capable of playing at right-back or in the middle of defence he made his Wanderers' debut as a substitute in the League Cup Final against Liverpool at Wembley. He returned there the following month to play his part in the play-off win against Reading. Since then he has missed very few games and scored a number of vital goals, perhaps none more enjoyable than the one against Spurs at White Hart Lane which earned the Wanderers their first away point in the Premier League. In 1996/97 he captained the Wanderers to the First Division championship and has at the time of writing appeared in 129 first team games. One of the biggest bargains in the club's history, he is also the most capped Icelandic international after making his seventy-fifth appearance in the summer of 1997.

CHAPTER SIX

THE GROUNDS

Last Premiership game at Burnden Park, 27 April 1996.

Among the early grounds used by the Wanderers were the Park Recreation Ground and Dick Cockle's field on Pikes Lane, opposite the Cross Guns pub. It was in 1874 that the newly formed Christ Church FC first played on these grounds but three years later, following a row with the Christ Church vicar, the club broke away under the name of Bolton Wanderers.

In March 1881 the club moved to a ground just off Pikes Lane. The ground had two small stands and shallow banking around a cinder track, but was notoriously very muddy and suffered from being at the foot of a hill from where an excellent free view was to be had!

In February 1884 *Athletic News* reported that between 4,000 and 5,000 spectators had assembled on the slopes during Bolton's FA Cup replay against Notts County and an enterprising farmer charged them half the Pikes Lane entrance fee! The annual rent for the ground in 1888 had been £35 but five years later, with Bolton now enjoying higher gates, the landlord increased the rent to £175. The club began to look for a more suitable site, and so Pikes Lane was last used in 1894/95.

The Wanderers wound up League football at Pikes Lane in grand fashion. Cup finalists and eventual winners Aston Villa were beaten 4–3, Nottingham Forest were defeated 4–1 and on Good Friday West Bromwich Albion were drubbed 5–0 with Peter Turnbull grabbing a second-half hat-trick.

The new site at Burnden was a former chemical works, bordered by a railway embankment and viaduct over the River Croal and a line of cottages along Manchester Road. A Scarborough contractor was called in to lay out the new ground under instructions from John Norris, one of the club's directors, who specifically requested a cycling track round the pitch, just like the one laid for the King of Italy!

Burnden Park was opened on 17 August 1895 with an athletics meeting, the town's ninth Annual Athletics Festival, attended by an impressive crowd of almost 20,000. Between events the enthusiastic audience were treated to a high-diver, a performer on stilts and a monkey on a bicycle!

On Wednesday 11 September 1895 the ground was eventually put to its proper use when Preston North End were the visitors for a benefit game for Di Jones. The crowd of 3,000 saw North End win the game with a solitary goal from David Smith. Three days later the first League game took place at Burnden Park with Everton as the visitors. The game was preceded by a cycle race an hour before the kick-off, witnessed by a 10,000 crowd which grew to 15,000 by 4 p.m. – the advertised start – and Bolton won the game 3–1.

However, over the next few weeks the pitch, which had been laid upon barrels of cotton bales, became such a quagmire that the reserves had to play one of their games at Pikes Lane, and in one match Preston North End refused to come out for the second half after a sudden downpour had flooded the playing area. To cure this problem, the drainage was improved by increasing the pitch's camber in 1896.

It wasn't too long before Burnden Park began to attract some important games and in April 1901 it was chosen as the venue for the FA Cup Final replay between Tottenham Hotspur and Sheffield United. A crowd of 50,000 had been expected but only 20,470 turned up, owing to a lack of cheap railway facilities. The occasion became known as 'Pie Saturday' on account of the catering miscalculations.

The club's run to the 1904 FA Cup Final helped finance the building of the Main Stand at a cost of £3,500. A year later the club won promotion to the First Division and after having their lease extended by ten years also had the cycle track removed to make room for the now much larger attendances. In 1906 the Great Lever End was terraced and covered, and after the club had purchased the freehold on the ground in 1914 a wing was added to the Main Stand. After the club's second FA Cup win in the 1920s, the old Darcy Lever Stand was replaced by the new Burnden Stand, seating 2,750.

Burnden Park's official highest crowd was 69,912 for the visit of Manchester City in the FA Cup in February 1933. During the Second World War the ground was taken over, the pitch for use by the Education Authorities and the stands by the Ministry of Supply. The Burnden Stand was still full of food supplies when the event which was to stand out in the history of all football grounds occurred on 9 March 1946, during Bolton's FA Cup tie against Stoke.

As the game began hundreds spilled out on to the track but it was not until 12 minutes later that it became apparent that there had been fatalities – thirty-three bodies were found and laid out on the pitch while first aid was given to a hundred. After the government report in 1947 the club spent £5,500 modernising the Railway End, improving the turnstiles and gates, adding barriers and fencing off the railway line.

On 14 October 1957 Bolton's new floodlights were switched on for a friendly against Hearts. It was claimed that they possessed sufficient power to light the streets from Burnden to Blackpool. Despite the club's fall from the top flight during the 1960s, Burnden hosted two FA Cup semi-finals. The post-war crowd record at Burnden came in February 1959 when 58,692 were at a fifth round FA Cup tie against Preston North End, and even as recently as 1977 the ground housed 50,413 for the League Cup semi-final second leg against Everton.

During the summer of 1979, 4,342 seats were put on the Great Lever End and the pitch, a poor drainer despite its camber, was dug up. All manner of compressed rotting matter was found underneath. Undersoil heating and sprinklers were installed, though at one stage it seemed inevitable that a plastic pitch would be laid at Burnden. This was vetoed by the Football League ruling that banned all further pitches of that nature for three years.

The greatest change took place in 1986 when the 16,000 Railway End terrace was cut in half by a Normid Superstore built in the north-west corner of the Embankment on the very spot that had seen the disaster.

After the Taylor Report reduced Burnden's capacity to 22,616 in 1995, the club decided to cut its losses at Burnden and relocate to a new site in Lostock. Thus Bolton's last game at Burnden Park was on 25 April 1996 when they beat Charlton Athletic 4–1.

The new 25,000 all-seater Reebok Stadium, which was constructed to FIFA and UEFA recommendations, provides some of the finest spectator facilities to be found anywhere in Europe – at a cost of £35 million. Adjoining the Reebok Stadium is the Middlebrook Development where over 3,000 jobs have been created.

The spectators at the Reebok are accommodated in lower and upper tiers, and because of the sweeping curves of the upper tier no one is ever seated more than 90 metres from the centre of the playing area. The Stadium has 46 executive box suites and the eight spectator concourses have concession units selling fans a variety of foods that can be consumed in view of one of the play-back TV screens in operation around the ground.

The reception foyer houses two lifts which will take guests up to three different floors where corporate executive areas can cater for over 2,000 people on match days.

The Pikes Lane ground pictured with the moors in the background.

A view from the embankment at Burnden Park taken in 1976.

A view of a snow-covered Burnden Park taken from the Manchester Road Stand.

The last Premiership game to be played at Burnden Park against Southampton on 27 April 1996 – notice the infamous Normid Superstore!

In the beginning – the site of the Reebok Stadium – the playing area is fenced off.

The entrance to the main reception area at the Reebok Stadium.

An aerial view of the Wanderers' new ground – the magnificent Reebok Stadium.

CHAPTER SEVEN

MEMORABLE MATCHES

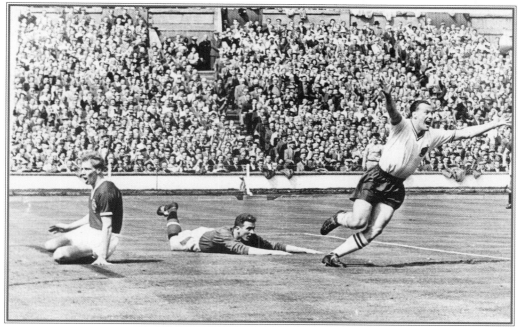

The legendary Lofthouse scores against Manchester United at Wembley, 1958.

Bolton Wanderers	0–1	**Manchester City**
FA Cup Final 23 April 1904		
Bolton Wanderers	2–0	**West Ham United**
FA Cup Final 28 April 1923		
Bolton Wanderers	1–0	**Manchester City**
FA Cup Final 24 April 1926		
Bolton Wanderers	2–0	**Portsmouth**
FA Cup Final 27 April 1929		
Bolton Wanderers	3–4	**Blackpool**
FA Cup Final 2 May 1953		
Bolton Wanderers	2–1	**Wolves**
FA Cup 6th Round 1 March 1958		
Bolton Wanderers	2–0	**Manchester United**
FA Cup Final 3 May 1958		
Bolton Wanderers	3–2	**Stoke City**
FA Cup 3rd Round 6 January 1974		
Bolton Wanderers	3–3	**Newcastle United**
FA Cup 5th Round 14 February 1976		
Bolton Wanderers	0–1	**Everton**
League Cup Semi-Final 15 February 1977		
Manchester United	1–2	**Bolton Wanderers**
League Division One 11 April 1979		
Bolton Wanderers	8–1	**Walsall**
League Division Three 10 September 1983		
Bolton Wanderers	0–3	**Bristol City**
Freight Rover Final 24 May 1986		
Bolton Wanderers	4–1	**Torquay United**
Sherpa Van Final 28 May 1989		
Bolton Wanderers	0–1	**Tranmere Rovers**
Play-Off Final 1 June 1991		
Liverpool	0–2	**Bolton Wanderers**
FA Cup 3rd Round Replay 13 January 1993		
Arsenal	1–3	**Bolton Wanderers**
FA Cup 4th Round Replay 9 February 1994		
Bolton Wanderers	1–2	**Liverpool**
League Cup Final 2 April 1995		
Bolton Wanderers	4–3	**Reading**
Play-Off Final 29 May 1995		
Bolton Wanderers	4–1	**Charlton Athletic**
League Division One 25 April 1997		
Bolton Wanderers	0–0	**Everton**
Premier League 1 September 1997		

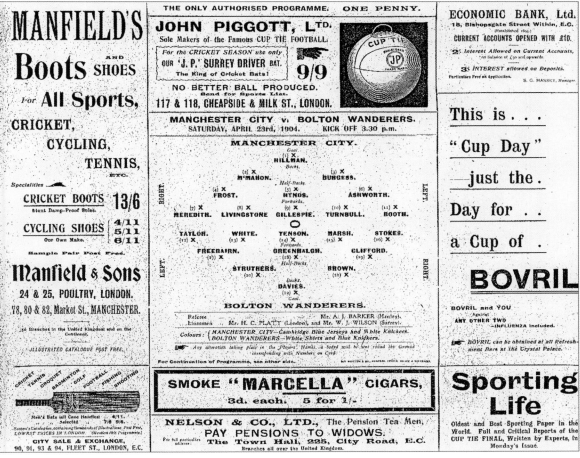

MANCHESTER CITY v. BOLTON WANDERERS.
SATURDAY, APRIL 23rd, 1904.   KICK OFF 3.30 p.m.

MANCHESTER CITY.

Goal
(1) X
HILLMAN.

Backs.
(2) X   (3) X
M'MAHON.   BURGESS.

Half-Backs.
(4) X   (5) X   (6) X
FROST.   HYNDS.   ASHWORTH.

Forwards.
(7) X   (8) X   (9) X   (10) X   (11) X
MEREDITH.   LIVINGSTONE. GILLESPIE. TURNBULL.   BOOTH.

O

(12) X   (13) X   (14) X   (15) X   (16) X
TAYLOR.   WHITE.   YENSON.   MARSH.   STOKES.

(17) X   (18) X   (19) X
FREEBAIRN.   GREENHALGH.   CLIFFORD.

Half-Backs.
(20) X   (21) X
STRUTHERS.   BROWN.

Backs.
(22) X
DAVIES.
Goal.

BOLTON WANDERERS.

Referee   Mr. A. J. BARKER (Hanley).
Linesmen   Mr. H. C. PLATT (London), and Mr. W. J. WILSON (Surrey).

Colours: { MANCHESTER CITY—Cambridge Blue Jerseys and White Knickers.
{ BOLTON WANDERERS—White Shirts and Blue Knickers.

Any alteration taking place in the Players' Names, a board will be sent round the Ground corresponding with Numbers on Card.

For Continuation of Programme, see other side.

The programme cover for the 1904 FA Cup Final against Manchester City. This was Bolton's second appearance in an FA Cup Final, having lost 4–1 to Second Division Notts County ten years earlier. This time the roles were reversed, for the Wanderers were in Division Two and City chasing the First Division Championship. The only goal of an otherwise dull game was controversial to say the least. City's Welsh international winger, the great Billy Meredith, was standing a good 2 yards behind Bolton's Bob Struthers in an offside position before receiving the ball and racing clear to shoot past Davies in the Bolton goal. After the interval Bolton were in charge, but despite creating a number of goalscoring opportunities they couldn't hit the target.

Bolton captain Joe Smith shakes hands with George Kay of West Ham United in the presence of referee D.H. Asson prior to the start of the 1923 FA Cup Final. This was Wembley's first full final and it nearly became a disaster. Though 126,047 people paid for admission, thousands more broke down the doors to invade the stadium. It is believed that almost 200,000 were present at kick-off time when the pitch was completely covered by spectators!

As the Bolton players stood on the edge of the pitch watching the police horse clear the playing area, someone tapped John Reid Smith on the back; it was his brother, whom he hadn't seen for six years! It was largely owing to the patience of the famous policeman on his white horse that the pitch was cleared but even so, spectators still encroached on to the pitch during play. However, it was felt safer to play the game than to announce to the horde that the match would be postponed. Within two minutes of the eventual kick-off, which was delayed by 40 minutes, David Jack had scored for the Wanderers. Both teams remained on the pitch at half-time, and eight minutes after the break Bolton scored again. Taking a pass from Ted Vizard, John Smith rammed the ball home with his left foot with such force that it hit the crowd wedged behind the goal and rebounded on to the pitch.

A full house at Wembley. The official attendance was 126,047 though it was estimated that over 200,000 were inside the ground.

The crowd encroached on to the field of play even after the pitch had been cleared by the famous policeman on his white horse. However, it was decided that it was safer to continue the game than to announce to the crowd that the match was being postponed.

The first Wembley winners and FA Cup winners for the first time in the club's history. Here they line up at Burnden Park. Left to right: Eccles (Trainer), Seddon, Pym, Rowley, Finney, Jennings, Jack, Vizard, Nuttall, John Smith, Haworth, Butler and Joe Smith. Harry Nuttall was born in the house just visible behind the Manchester Road Stand.

1925/6.

Three Bolton international players, David Jack, Joe Smith and Dick Pym, were in the Bolton line-up for the 1926 FA Cup Final against Manchester City. In what turned out to be one of the most sporting FA Cup Finals of all time, the Wanderers gained revenge for their defeat at the hands of City in the 1904 final. In quite a one-sided game the Wanderers were guilty of a number of missed chances, though City's former Bolton player, Frank Roberts, did force Dick Pym into one memorable save early in the second half. The only goal of the game came in the 78th minute when Welsh international winger Ted Vizard crossed for David Jack to shoot home from close range. City then pushed forward in numbers and only the alertness of Pym in the Bolton goal prevented the Maine Road club from equalising.

Bolton's Bob Haworth and Dick Pym in goalmouth action as the Wanderers faced Portsmouth in their third Wembley FA Cup Final in seven seasons, with six of their side having already experienced the occasion. Despite this, it was Portsmouth that did the bulk of the attacking in a goalless first half.

Bolton seemed to be the more solid team and were playing well within themselves and not forcing the pace. One of the reasons for these carefully pre-planned tactics was the fact that Wanderers' 'keeper Dick Pym was carrying an injury sustained before the Final. The Wanderers took the lead in the 78th minute when Billy Butler crashed home a powerful shot past the bemused Gilfillan in the Pompey goal. Within a minute Harold Blackmore, who ended the season with 37 goals, netted Bolton's second to make the game safe and take the Cup back to Burnden Park for a third time that decade.

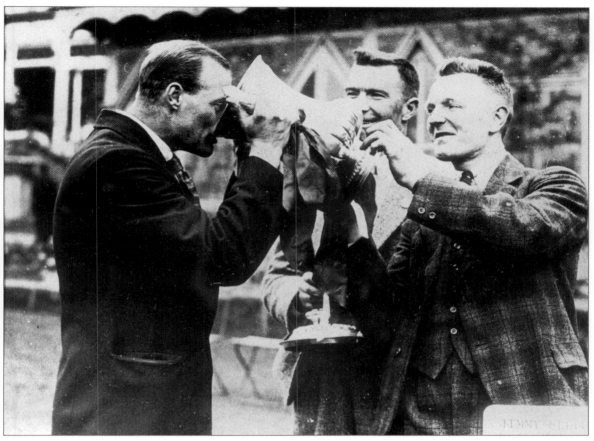

The Wanderers celebrate after beating Portsmouth 2–0 in the 1929 FA Cup Final. Jimmy Seddon drinks from the Cup, watched by team-mates Dick Pym and Harold Blackmore.

In one of the most exciting FA Cup Finals in history, Bolton took the lead after just 75 seconds when Nat Lofthouse (shown above) with an underhit shot from 28 yards deceived George Farm in the Blackpool goal. Even though a hamstring strain reduced left-half Eric Bell to a passenger on the wing, Bolton continued to pour forward and Lofthouse almost doubled the Wanderers' lead when his shot came back off a post. Stan Mortensen equalised for the Seasiders after 36 minutes but Bolton were back in front by the interval as Willie Moir scored with a glancing header from Bobby Langton's cross.

After the break Bolton extended their lead when the injured Bell threw himself forward to head home Holden's cross. With a 3–1 lead the destination of the Cup seemed settled, but with little over half-an-hour left Stanley Matthews took over.

The Seasiders pulled a goal back in the 68th minute when Mortensen forced the ball home from close range after Hanseon had failed to hold Matthews' shot. With just one minute remaining, Mortensen struck home a free kick from outside the Bolton penalty area and then created the winner for Bill Perry two minutes into injury time.

Nat Lofthouse, Bolton Wanderers and England. A local boy who made good with his local club, Nat shares with Tom Finney the record number of goals for England (30), has led England all over the world, and skippered Bolton to their last F.A. Cup Final triumph

In one of the most exciting FA Cup ties ever played at Burnden Park, Bolton took the lead after 27 minutes when Birch's cross was converted by Dennis Stevens who shot high into the roof of the net past the despairing dive of Wolves' 'keeper Finlayson. However, within two minutes the Molineux side were level when Bobby Mason flicked home Norman Deeley's cross.

Ten minutes into the second half Lofthouse chased a long through ball from Derek Hennin, but as Finlayson came out to dive at the centre-forward's feet he handled the ball outside the 18-yard line. From the resultant free kick Ray Parry curved the ball into the net past the flat-footed Wolves' 'keeper to put Bolton 2–1 up. Wolves then threw caution to the winds and tore relentlessly into Bolton. They hit the Bolton posts and crossbar on half a dozen occasions, while both Hartle and Banks cleared shots off the line. Sadly Bolton's goalscoring hero, Ray Parry, was stretchered off near the end following an accidental collision with Finlayson.

Bolton Evening News FA Cup Sixth Round special to commemorate the match between Bolton Wanderers and Wolverhampton Wanderers at Burnden Park on 1 March 1958.

Nat Lofthouse scores Bolton's opening goal against Manchester United in the 1958 FA Cup Final at Wembley.

Manager Bill Ridding, trainer Bert Sproston and coaches George Taylor and George Hunt with the FA Cup after Bolton's 2–0 win over Manchester United in the 1958 final.

Harry Gregg, one of the Munich air crash survivors, is tended by one of his team-mates after being knocked out during the 1958 FA Cup Final. Having led the Wanderers to Wembley for the second time in five years, Bill Ridding, whose side cost no more than the £10 signing-on fee, faced a Manchester United side rebuilding after the Munich tragedy.

Bolton took the lead as early as the third minute when Nat Lofthouse stabbed the ball home from 5 yards out after a speculative ball from Bryan Edwards was deflected into his path. Though the Wanderers were the better side, two shots from Bobby Charlton, one that hit the inside of a post and one that brought a magnificent save out of Eddie Hopkinson, reminded Bolton that the game wasn't yet won. Then in the 57th minute came Bolton's second goal, one of the most controversial in Cup Final history. Dennis Stevens fired in a shot that United 'keeper Harry Gregg could only push vertically into the air, and as he turned and jumped to gather the ball, Lofthouse bundled both Gregg and the ball over the line. Unbelievably by today's standards, the referee signalled a goal and though it was at a time when goalkeepers were considered fair game, many neutral observers believed it was a foul!

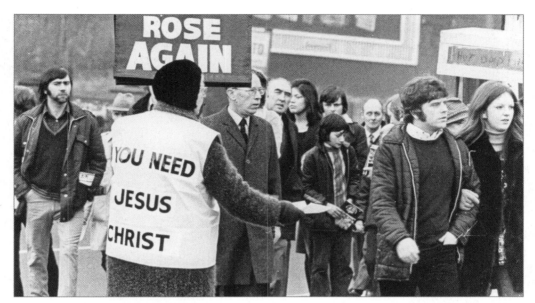

Sunday football comes to Burnden Park when the Wanderers entertain Stoke City in an FA Cup third round match on 6 January 1974 – not everyone is happy!

Once the Burnden officials heard that the FA were ready to countenance Sunday football, they quickly got to grips with rearranging their third round tie against Stoke City and created history into the bargain, being the first club to exploit the political situation of a three-day week to their advantage. An attendance of 39,138 gave the experiment the fans' seal of approval and John Byrom, who was at his goalscoring best, made sure Wanderers profited from the exercise.

He grabbed a sensational hat-trick – a header, a smart finish after a solo run and an audacious flick and half-volley (shown above). Three up with just 30 minutes to play, the Wanderers appeared to have the tie in the bag, but First Division Stoke refused to lie down and pulled goals back from Ritchie and Haselgrove. Just when it seemed the Potters would equalise, Byrom turned up on his own goal-line to clear the danger and turn to salute the Bolton fans!

Garry Jones and Neil Whatmore celebrate Bolton's second goal in one of the most exciting FA Cup ties of the post-war era. Sam Allardyce gave the Wanderers a fifth-minute lead against League Cup finalists Newcastle United. Garry Jones missed a golden opportunity in the 18th minute to put Bolton 2–0 up before England international Malcolm MacDonald equalised for the Magpies on the half-hour. On the stroke of half-time MacDonald gave Newcastle the lead with a magnificent goal. With his back to the Bolton goal he turned, dummied past Paul Jones and sent a superb right-foot 'bender' into the top corner of Barry Siddall's net from fully 30 yards.

Garry Jones levelled the scores six minutes into the second half, but with just eight minutes to go Alan Gowling, who was later to join the Wanderers, ran through the heart of the Bolton defence before shooting past a hapless Siddall. There were just three minutes remaining when Paul Jones met a Roy Greaves' corner and powered home a header that went through MacDonald's legs and over the goal-line for Wanderers' last-gasp equaliser. After a goalless draw at St James's Park, the Magpies won through to the quarter-finals with a 2–1 win at Elland Road.

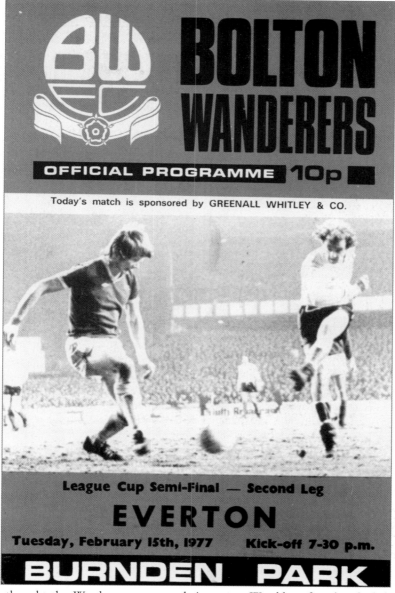

Bolton fans thought the Wanderers were on their way to Wembley after they had drawn 1–1 at Goodison Park in the first leg of the League Cup semi-final against Everton. A crowd of 50,413 crammed into Burnden Park but unfortunately the Wanderers couldn't get their game together. The only goal of the game came in the 23rd minute when Ronnie Goodlass crossed for Bob Latchford to head past Jim McDonagh in the Bolton goal. Bolton's only real clear-cut chance on a night when they struggled to find any rhythm fell to Neil Whatmore who lobbed the ball over the bar with David Lawson stranded. The Toffees had the chance to extend their lead in the 65th minute when they were awarded a penalty following Sam Allardyce's clumsy challenge on Duncan McKenzie. McKenzie picked himself up but drove his spot-kick wide of McDonagh's right-hand post. There were just two minutes remaining when Willie Morgan forced the ball home, but he was given offside and with that went Wanderers' hopes of a Wembley appearance.

WHICH WAY DID IT GO ? Frank Worthington sends Manchester United Gary Bailey the wrong way to score in the Wanderers 2-1 win at Old Trafford.

Picture by Bolton Evening News

Frank Worthington scored both Bolton's goals in this game as the Wanderers completed a memorable fight-back. United opened the scoring in the first half through a headed goal by Martin Buchan but though they laid siege to the Bolton goal, the Trotters' defence soaked up everything the Reds could throw at them.

Worthington levelled the scores in the 53rd minute when he converted his 23rd goal of the season, but as United attacked the Bolton defence finally cracked when Paul Jones handled Sammy McIlroy's cross. Gordon McQueen sent Jim McDonagh the wrong way but referee Pat Partridge adjudged that a United player had encroached into the penalty area and ordered the kick to be retaken. This time McQueen's shot hit the inside of the post, rolled across the face of the goal and out for a goal-kick. There were just seconds remaining when Brian Smith broke away from the United defence and crossed for Worthington to his second and Bolton's winner.

Wanderers' part-time forward Tony Caldwell set a new club record in this Third Division match by scoring five goals in an 8–1 win over Walsall. Winger Jeff Chandler helped set up Caldwell's first two goals in the 18th and 22nd minutes and had a hand in the third Bolton goal scored by captain Ray Deakin. Caldwell completed his hat-trick on the stroke of half-time and then netted his fourth (seen above) and fifth goals in the 59th and 75th minutes.

Walsall then came back into the game as Bolton pushed forward in search of further goals, but both Brown and Summerfield missed easy chances. Simon Rudge netted Bolton's seventh goal before centre-half Peter Valentine fired home from 25 yards to put Bolton 8–0 up. Just when it seemed as if the Wanderers would score nine, Ally Brown netted a consolation for the Saddlers in the dying seconds.

Mark Gavin fires in a shot in the Freight Rover Trophy Final against Bristol City, but sadly the Wanderers' sixth visit to Wembley ends in their heaviest defeat in a major Cup Final. Though the better side on the day won, it could have been a different story if Tony Caldwell's shot early in the first half had gone in instead of hitting the bar. The Ashton Gate club took the lead just before half-time when Simon Farnworth's punch-out landed at the feet of Glyn Riley and his shot beat Mark Came's desperate goal-line clearance. City's second goal came in the 73rd minute when Farnworth palmed out Neville's shot to Howard Pritchard who hit the ball high into the roof of the net. As Bolton pushed forward they left gaps at the back and this allowed Riley to head home a third goal.

The Sherpa Van Trophy Final saw the Wanderers go a goal behind to Fourth Division Torquay United in front of a Wembley crowd of 46,513. Julian Darby (above), the only Bolton-born player in the Wanderers' side, equalised in the 27th minute when he turned and hit a low right-foot shot past the despairing dive of the Devon club's 'keeper, Kenny Allen.

Bolton took the lead in the 63rd minute when Jeff Chandler's shot took a deflection off Torquay defender John Morrison and left Allen stranded. Torquay pushed forward in search of an equaliser and it took two brilliant one-handed saves from Bolton's Welsh international 'keeper Dave Felgate to keep United's forwards at bay. The Wanderers then scored two goals in the space of three minutes to put the game beyond Torquay's reach. Dean Crombie scored his first-ever goal for the club when he raced clear to chip the ball over the advancing Allen. Then in the 82nd minute Trevor Morgan converted substitute Stuart Storer's cross to give Bolton the trophy and establish a new club record of 20 games without defeat.

Having failed to pip Grimsby Town for the third promotion spot in Division Three, the Wanderers went into the play-offs where they met Bury who had finished ten points adrift of their rivals. In the first leg at Gigg Lane the game ended all-square at 1–1 with both goals coming from the penalty spot, David Lee netting for Bury and Tony Philliskirk for the Wanderers. It was Phillsikirk who scored the only goal of the second leg at Burnden Park to take the Wanderers through to the play-off final against Tranmere Rovers at Wembley.

It seemed that the semi-final tie had taken too much out of the Bolton side, who appeared to be physically drained on the day. Both teams had chances to open the scoring, perhaps the best to Stuart Storer (in action above as he beats off the challenge of Tranmere's Ged Brannan), but after 90 minutes the game was goalless and went into extra time. Tranmere's Chris Malkin scored the game's only goal to condemn the Wanderers to another season of Third Division football, after ending the 1990/91 season five points ahead of their Birkenhead opponents.

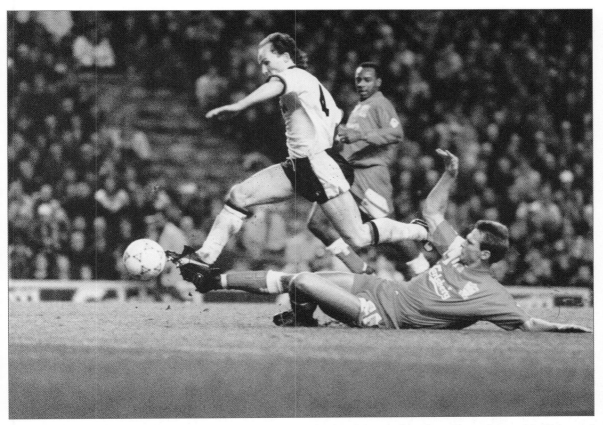

In the first meeting between Bolton and Liverpool on a Sunday lunchtime in bitterly cold conditions, McGinlay and Seagraves had given the Wanderers a 2–0 lead at half-time against their Premier League opponents. The Reds hit back after the interval with an own goal by Mark Winstanley and an equaliser by Ian Rush, just eight minutes from time.

In the replay at Anfield the Wanderers completely outplayed the cup holders, and took the lead after just three minutes when David Lee (pictured above) crossed for John McGinlay to head home. In the second half both Andy Walker and Scott Green hurried their shots when they had more time to steady themselves, but with 12 minutes left the Wanderers added a second. McGinlay crossed from the right wing and Andy Walker was there to head past Mike Hooper in the Liverpool goal to send the 9,000 Bolton fans in the 34,790 crowd wild with delight.

After knocking the cup holders out of the competition last season the Wanderers had the chance to repeat the feat. Arsenal were the visitors to Burnden Park for this FA Cup fourth round tie, a game in which the 18,891 crowd certainly got their money's worth for sheer entertainment value. McAteer opened the scoring for Bolton before goals from Ian Wright and Tony Adams gave the Gunners the lead. There were just four minutes left when Owen Coyle volleyed McGinlay's header into the roof of the net for the equaliser.

In the replay at Highbury John McGinlay (seen above) headed the Wanderers into the lead in the 20th minute, and though Alan Smith equalised for the Gunners to take the tie into extra time Bolton had been the better team. It was the Wanderers who took the lead when Jason McAteer fired home the rebound after Owen Coyle's shot had struck the upright. Andy Walker added a third when he fired low under the body of England 'keeper David Seaman, and Tony Kelly had what appeared a perfectly good goal disallowed for offside. Martin Keown was later sent off for a second bookable offence as the Wanderers beat an Arsenal side who were to win that season's European Cup Winners' Cup 3–1.

After beating Swindon Town 4–3 on aggregate in the semi-final of the Coca Cola Cup, the Wanderers faced Liverpool at Wembley in their first major Cup Final for 37 years. The Wanderers came close to getting the all-important first goal when Thompson's spectacular right foot volley had David James at full stretch and David Lee's lob beat the stranded Liverpool 'keeper for the ball to drop just over the crossbar. The Reds took the lead when Steve McManaman's run took him past Stubbs and Green before stroking a shot wide of Keith Branagan's right leg.

Early in the second half Mixu Paatelainen's shot went just wide of the post before Stig Bjornebye hit Keith Branagan's left-hand post. McManaman then made Green pay for an ill-timed tackle, cut inside Mark Seagraves and curled a right-footed shot just out of Branagan's reach. With Jason McAteer (above) always in the thick of the action, the Wanderers pushed forward and Gudni Bergsson, who replaced Scott Green, set up the Wanderers' goal for Alan Thompson, whose chest control, turn and flashing left foot volley shot into James' top right-hand corner.

After a nail-biting conclusion to the 1994/95 season, the Wanderers celebrate after beating Reading 4-3 after extra time in the play-off final, to put the club into the top flight after 15 years in the wilderness. But after a lacklustre first half victory looked a distant dream, especially after the Wanderers had gone 2–0 down in the opening quarter of an hour. In fact Reading were awarded a penalty in the 35th minute but a superb save from Keith Branagan kept the Wanderers in the game. In the second half Bolton came out fighting, outclassing the Reading side as they launched wave after wave of attack on the Berkshire club's goal. The Wanderers' determination was rewarded when Owen Coyle headed home 14 minutes from the final whistle and then, with just three minutes of normal time remaining, Fabian de Freitas equalised to take the game to extra time. Jason McAteer crossed for Mixu Paatelainen to head over Shaka Hislop to put the Wanderers 3–2 up and then de Freitas scrambled the ball past the Reading 'keeper after he had saved his first shot. Reading player-manager Jimmy Quinn reduced the arrears in the dying seconds. It was a gutsy fightback by the Wanderers that clinched a place among the top flight of football's élite.

The Wanderers signed off in style as the curtain came down on 102 years of football at Burnden Park and are seen above celebrating winning the First Division championship after beating Charlton Athletic. Charlton certainly made it difficult for Bolton, and Mark Kinsella's 18th minute spectacular 25-yard shot that whistled past Keith Branagan silenced the 22,030 crowd. However, no-one was going to spoil this party, and after Alan Thompson equalised in the first minute of the second half it was all one-way traffic. Gerry Taggert crashed home an unstoppable volley that put the Bolton fans in sight of the victory the occasion merited before two late goals from John McGinlay, the first a penalty, put the result beyond doubt. Bolton manager Colin Todd sent up Bergsson, McGinlay and Taggert to receive the 108-year-old trophy, formerly the coveted prize of the English League champions, while Nat Lofthouse and Chairman Gordon Hargreaves dug up the centre-spot in a symbolic transfer of the Burnden spirit to the new Reebok Stadium.

The Reebok Stadium staged its first-ever game when the Wanderers entertained Everton in the Premier League and Sky TV cameras were there to record the historic event. Fans paid silent tribute to Diana, Princess of Wales, before the game, the crowd of 23,131 solemnly observing a one-minute silence before kick-off. Unfortunately the game failed to match the event and tragedy struck when Robbie Elliott, Bolton's £3.5 million signing from Newcastle United, was stretchered off with a broken leg. Though the game was goalless, the Wanderers did actually get the ball over Neville Southall's goal-line when in the 54th minute Gerry Taggert's header looped over the Welsh international 'keeper and dropped over the Everton line before full-back Terry Phelan hacked it away (above). To everyone's amazement, the referee waved play on, and though Nathan Blake later spurned a good chance there wasn't another worthwhile scoring effort from either side.

APPENDICES

HONOURS
Football League

Division 1	Champions	1996/97		
Division 2	Champions	1908/09	1977/78	
	Runners-Up	1899/1900	1904/05	1910/11
		1934/35	1992/93	
Division 3	Champions	1972/73		
FA Cup	Winners	1923	1926	1929
		1958		
	Runners-Up	1894	1904	1953
League Cup	Runners-Up	1995		
Sherpa Van	Winners	1989		
Freight Rover	Runners-Up	1986		

LONGEST LEAGUE RUNS

Of undefeated matches	23	(13 October 1990 – 9 March 1991)
Of undefeated home matches	27	(24 April 1920 – 24 September 1921)
Without a home win	11	(19 April 1902 – 10 January 1903)
Of league wins	11	(5 November 1904 – 2 January 1905)
Of league defeats	11	(7 April 1902 – 18 October 1902)
League matches without a win	26	(7 April 1902 – 10 January 1903)
Of undefeated away matches	11	(10 December 1904 – 21 April 1905)
Without an away win	36	(25 Sept 1948 – 2 September 1950)
Of home wins	17	(11 October 1924 – 25 April 1925)
Of away wins	5	(10 December 1904 – 18 March 1905)

CLUB RECORDS

Most home wins in a season	18	(1924/25 1972/73 1992/93 1996/97)
Most home draws in a season	11	(1979/80)
Most home defeats in a season	10	(1909/10 1963/64 1970/71 1986/87 1995/96)
Most home goals scored in a season	63	(1934/35)
Most home goals conceded in a season	35	(1952/53 1957/58 1963/64)
Least home wins in a season	5	(1979/80 1995/96)
Least home draws in a season	0	(1888/89 1890/91 1904/05)
Least home defeats in a season	0	(1910/11 1920/21)
Least home goals scored in a season	16	(1995/96)
Least home goals conceded in a season	7	(1899/1900)
Most away wins in a season	12	(1904/05)
Most away draws in a season	10	(1986/87 1996/97)
Most away defeats in a season	18	(1984/85)
Most away goals scored in a season	40	(1996/97)
Most away goals conceded in a season	59	(1932/33)
Least away wins in a season	0	(1949/50 1979/80)
Least away draws in a season	0	(1889/90 1891/92)
Least away defeats in a season	3	(1899/1900 1904/05 1996/97)

Least away goals scored in a season	10	(1897/98)
Least away goals conceded in a season	16	(1904/05)
Most wins in a season	28	(1996/97)
Most draws in a season	17	(1991/92)
Most defeats in a season	25	(1970/71 1995/96)
Most goals scored in a season	100	(1996/97)
Most goals conceded in a season	92	(1932/33)
Least wins in a season	5	(1979-80)
Least draws in a season	1	(1889/90 1890/91)
Least defeats in a season	4	(1899/1900 1996/97)
Least goals scored in a season	28	(1897/98)
Least goals conceded in a season	25	(1899/1900)

APPEARANCES

	F. Lg	FA Cup	F.Lg Cup	Others	Total
E. Hopkinson	519	38	21	0	578
R. Greaves	487/8	39	41	0	567/8
A. Finney	483	47	0	0	530
W. Rimmer	462/7	30	29	0	521/7
B. Edwards	482	31	5	0	518
T. Vizard	467	45	0	0	512
N. Lofthouse	452	49	2	0	503
P. Jones	441/4	31	30	0	502/4
R. Hartle	446/1	39	13	0	498/1
J. Smith	449	43	0	0	492
D. Holden	419	40	4	0	463
B. Butler	407	42	0	0	449
S. Hanson	384	39	0	0	423
D. Stokes	387	33	0	0	420
S. Thompson	329/6	21	27	39	416/6
F. Hill	373/2	23	14	0	410/2
S. Farrimond	364/1	22	17	0	403/1
H. Baverstock	366	22	0	0	388
J. Ritson	321/3	30	24	0	375/3
J. Seddon	337	38	0	0	375

GOALSCORERS

	F. Lg	FA Cup	F.Lg Cup	Others	Total
N. Lofthouse	255	27	3	0	285
J. Smith	254	23	0	0	277
D. Jack	144	17	0	0	161
J. Milsom	142	11	0	0	153
R. Westwood	127	17	0	0	144
W. Moir	118	16	0	0	134
J. Byrom	113	7	10	0	130
H. Blackmore	111	11	0	0	122
N. Whatmore	107	7	7	0	121
J. McGinlay	87	10	14	7	118

F. Lee	92	8	6	0	106
J. Cassidy	84	17	0	0	101
D. Stevens	90	9	2	0	101
W. White	88	5	0	0	93
A. Shepherd	85	5	0	0	90
J. R. Smith	72	15	0	0	87
R. Greaves	66	10	9	0	85
G. Gibson	76	5	0	0	81
S. Marsh	72	9	0	0	81
F. Roberts	79	1	0	0	80

MANAGERS' FOOTBALL LEAGUE RECORDS

	P	W	D	L	F	A
John Somerville	60	28	6	26	85	73
Will Settle	206	89	44	73	336	308
Charles Foweraker	840	338	211	291	1442	1277
Walter Rowley	180	58	39	83	229	279
Bill Ridding	714	269	171	274	1124	1118
Nat Lofthouse	113	30	33	50	138	176+
Jimmy McIlroy	2	0	0	2	0	3
Jimmy Meadows	11	1	3	7	6	25
Jimmy Armfield	142	59	41	42	175	129
Ian Greaves	226	90	63	73	310	274
Stan Anderson	60	18	16	26	83	97
George Mulhall	42	13	7	22	39	61
John McGovern	111	36	24	51	133	156
Charlie Wright	39	10	7	22	42	67
Phil Neal	309	115	93	101	381	355
Bruce Rioch	141	65	37	39	217	155
Roy McFarland	21	2	4	15	19	40
Colin Todd	101	43	28	30	161	145

EVER-PRESENTS

	Season	Top League Scorers	
J. Brogan, J. Milne, D. Weir, R. Roberts, J. Davenport	1888/89	J. Brogan	13
	1889/90	J. Cassidy	13
J. McNee, A. Paton	1890/91	J. McNee	9
J. McNee, A. Paton, D. Jones J. Cassidy, H. Gardiner J. Sutcliff,e J. Somerville	1891/92	J. Cassidy	18
A. Paton, J. Sutcliffe, D. Jones	1892/93	J. Cassidy J. Dickenson	9 9
	1893/94	J. Cassidy	11
A. Paton	1894/95	C. Henderson	14
A. Paton, A. Freebairn J. Wright	1895/96	W. Joyce	12
A. Freebairn	1896/97	R. Jack	11

A. Freebairn	1897/98	J. Cassidy	7
	1898/99	A. Gilligan	6
		H. Morgan	6
	1899/1900	L. Bell	23
J. Picken	1900/01	L. Bell	8
		J. McKie	8
	1901/02	T.H. Barlow	10
	1902/03	S. Marsh	9
	1903/04	S. Marsh	16
	1904/05	S. Marsh	26
J. Boyd, D. Stokes, W. White	1905/06	A. Shepherd	26
H. Baverstock	1906/07	A. Shepherd	16
D. Stokes	1907/08	A. Shepherd	25
J. Edmondson	1908/09	W. Hughes	16
	1909/10	W. Hughes	12
	1910/11	W. Hughes	21
T. Barber	1911/12	J. Smith	22
	1912/13	J. Smith	22
	1913/14	G.R. Lillycrop	24
J. Smith, T. Vizard	1914/15	J. Smith	29
T. Buchan	1919/20	F. Roberts	26
F. Roberts	1920/21	J. Smith	38
	1921/22	D. Jack	28
D. Pym	1922/23	J. Smith	17
A. Finney	1923/24	D. Jack	24
D. Jack	1924/25	D. Jack	26
	1925/26	J. Smith	15
	1926/27	D. Jack	16
	1927/28	D. Jack	24
	1928/29	H. Blackmore	30
G. Gibson, R. Haworth	1929/30	H. Blackmore	30
	1930/31	H. Blackmore	27
R. Jones	1931/32	J. Milsom	19
	1932/33	J. Milsom	25
	1933/34	J. Milsom	23
H. Goslin, R. Smith, G.T. Taylor	1934/35	J. Milsom	31
G.T. Taylor	1935/36	J. Milsom	20
	1936/37	J. Milsom	13
	1937/38	R. Westwood	23
H. Goslin	1938/39	G.S. Hunt	23
L. Hamlett, S. Hanson	1946/47	N. Lofthouse	18
	1947/48	N. Lofthouse	18
W. Moir	1948/49	W. Moir	25
	1949/50	N. Lofthouse	10
S. Hanson, D. Howe	1950/51	N. Lofthouse	21
	1951/52	N. Lofthouse	18
S. Hanson	1952/53	N. Lofthouse	22
J. Ball, D. Holden	1953/54	W. Moir	18

J. Ball	1954/55	N. Lofthouse	15
B. Edwards	1955/56	N. Lofthouse	32
D. Holden, E. Hopkinson	1956/57	N. Lofthouse	28
B. Edwards			
J. Higgins	1957/58	N. Lofthouse	17
	1958/59	N. Lofthouse	29
D. Holden	1959/60	D. Stevens	14
E. Hopkinson	1960/61	B. McAdams	18
E. Hopkinson, B. Edwards	1961/62	F. Hill	14
W. Rimmer, S. Farrimond			
	1962/63	F. Lee	12
	1963/64	F. Lee	12
W. Rimmer, G. Taylor	1964/65	F. Lee	23
E. Hopkinson, W. Rimmer	1965/66	W. Davies	13
	1966/67	F. Lee	22
	1967/68	R. Greaves	10
E. Hopkinson	1968/69	R. Greaves	11
	1969/70	J. Byrom	20
	1970/71	R. Hunt	8
C. Wright	1971/72	J. Byrom, R. Hunt	11
P. Jones	1972/73	J. Byrom	20
B. Siddall	1973/74	J. Byrom	18
P. Jones, B. Siddall	1974/75	H. Curran	11
R. Greaves, P. Reid	1975/76	N. Whatmore	11
		G. Jones	11
P. Jones, P. Reid	1976/77	N. Whatmore	25
J. McDonagh, N. Whatmore	1977/78	N. Whatmore	19
J. McDonagh, M. Walsh	1978/79	F. Worthington	24
F. Worthington			
J. McDonagh, M. Walsh	1979/80	N. Whatmore	16
	1980/81	N. Whatmore	14
	1981/82	T. Henry	13
J. McDonagh	1982/83	T. Henry	9
J. Chandler	1983/84	T. Caldwell	19
S. Farnworth	1984/85	T. Caldwell	18
A. Hartford	1985/86	T. Caldwell	10
	1986/87	T. Caldwell	11
D. Felgate	1987/88	J. Thomas	22
D. Felgate, P. Brown	1988/89	T. Morgan	10
P. Brown, J. Darby	1989/90	T. Philliskirk	18
D. Felgate	1990/91	T. Philliskirk	19
	1991/92	A. Walker	15
K. Branagan	1992/93	A. Walker	26
J. McAteer	1993/94	J. McGinlay	25
J. Phillips	1994/95	J. McGinlay	16
	1995/96	J. McGinlay	6
C. Fairclough	1996/97	J. McGinlay	24
P. Frandsen	1997/98	N. Blake	12

HAT-TRICK HEROES

Player	Goals	Date	Comp	Opponents	Score
J. Turner	3	10. 11. 1888	FAC	West Manchester	9–0
D. Weir	3	22. 12. 1888	L	Accrington	4–1
J. Davenport	3	09. 03. 1889	L	Notts County	7–3
J. Cassidy	4	30. 11. 1889	L	Derby County	7–1
D. Weir	4	18. 01. 1890	FAC	Belfast Dist	10–2
J. Cassidy	5	01. 02. 1890	FAC	Sheffield United	13–0
D. Weir	4	01. 02. 1890	FAC	Sheffield United	13–0
J. Brogan	3	01. 02. 1890	FAC	Sheffield United	13–0
J. Cassidy	3	08. 02. 1890	L	Stoke	5–0
A. Barbour	3	03. 11. 1890	L	Accrington	6–0
J. McNee	3	29. 12. 1890	L	Wolves	6–0
J. Cassidy	3	18. 04. 1892	L	Everton	5–2
J. Cassidy	3	24. 09,1892	L	Aston Villa	5–0
J. Dickenson	3	15. 10. 1892	L	Stoke	4–4
D. Weir	3	04. 03. 1893	L	Accrington	5–2
C. Henderson	3	15. 12. 1894	L	Wolves	6–1
C. Henderson	4	01. 01. 1895	L	Derby County	6–0
P. Turnbull	3	13. 04. 1895	L	West Bromwich Albion	5–0
J. Hanson	3	26. 12. 1899	L	Barnsley	6–1
L. Bell	3	30. 12. 1899	L	Loughborough Town	7–0
T. McAteer	3	02. 01. 1900	L	Port Vale	5–0
L. Bell	4	28. 04. 1900	L	Burton Swifts	5–0
J. McKie	3	04. 01. 1902	L	Small Heath	4–0
S. Marsh	3	17. 10. 1903	L	Gainsborough Trinity	5–0
S. Marsh	3	25. 12. 1903	L	Barnsley	5–1
W. White	3	24. 09. 1904	L	Grimsby Town	4–1
S. Marsh	3	19. 11. 1904	L	Burton United	7–1
W. White	3	19. 11. 1904	L	Burton United	7–1
W. White	3	10. 12. 1904	L	Doncaster Rovers	4–0
A. Shepherd	4	18. 11. 1905	L	Nottingham Forest	6–0
A. Shepherd	4	17. 02. 1906	L	Sunderland	6–2
A. Shepherd	3	08. 09. 1906	L	Sheffield United	6–1
A. Shepherd	3	07. 09. 1907	L	Bury	3–6
W. White	3	12. 10. 1907	L	Chelsea	3–1
A. Shepherd	3	07. 12. 1907	L	Arsenal	3–1
S. Marsh	3	22. 02. 1908	FAC	Everton	3–3
A. Shepherd	3	01. 04. 1908	L	Newcastle United	4–0
B. Hughes	3	05. 09. 1910	L	West Bromwich Albion	3–1
B. Hughes	3	03. 12. 1910	L	Huddersfield Town	3–1
B. Hughes	3	24. 12. 1910	L	Birmingham	5–1
B. Hughes	3	31. 12. 1910	L	Leicester Fosse	6–2
J. Smith	4	03. 01. 1914	L	Manchester United	6–1
J. Smith	3	31. 01. 1914	FAC	Swindon Town	4–2
J. Smith	3	28. 03. 1914	L	Bradford City	3–0
J. Smith	4	26. 12. 1914	L	Aston Villa	7–1
J. Smith	3	17. 09. 1919	L	Middlesbrough	3–1

Player	Goals	Date	Comp	Opponents	Score
T. Buchan	3	25. 12. 1919	L	Preston North End	4–1
F. Roberts	3	07. 04. 1920	L	Aston Villa	6–3
J. Smith	3	30. 10. 1920	L	Middlesbrough	6–2
J. Smith	4	25. 12. 1920	L	Sunderland	6–2
J. Smith	3	09. 04. 1921	L	Newcastle United	3–1
D. Jack	3	02. 01. 1922	L	Oldham Athletic	5–1
D. Jack	3	09. 12. 1922	L	West Bromwich Albion	3–0
J.R. Smith	4	02. 01. 1923	L	Nottingham Forest	4–2
J.R. Smith	3	03. 09. 1923	L	Sheffield United	4–2
D. Jack	3	10. 11. 1923	L	Chelsea	4–0
D. Jack	3	26. 12. 1923	L	West Bromwich Albion	5–0
J.R. Smith	3	29. 11. 1924	L	West Ham United	5–0
J. Smith	3	28. 02. 1925	L	Manchester City	4–2
D. Jack	4	22. 04. 1925	L	Blackburn Rovers	6–0
T. Vizard	3	10. 10. 1925	L	Arsenal	3–2
J.R. Smith	3	01. 01. 1926	L	Birmingham	5–3
J.R. Smith	3	28. 08. 1926	L	Leeds United	5–2
B. Butler	3	25. 12. 1926	L	Derby County	3–1
J.R. Smith	3	08. 01. 1927	FAC	Blackpool	3–1
G. Gibson	3	16. 04. 1927	L	Everton	5–0
B. Wright	3	30. 04. 1927	L	Huddersfield Town	4–0
H. Blackmore	4	05. 11. 1927	L	Burnley	7–1
D. Jack	3	05. 11. 1927	L	Burnley	7–1
D. Jack	3	24. 12. 1927	L	Sheffield United	3–4
H. Blackmore	3	13. 10. 1928	L	Portsmouth	4–2
H. Blackmore	3	20. 10. 1928	L	Aston Villa	5–3
G. Gibson	3	27. 10. 1928	L	Sheffield United	3–1
H. Blackmore	3	26. 12. 1928	L	Birmingham	6–2
W. Cook	3	14. 12. 1929	L	West Ham United	4–1
H. Blackmore	4	28. 12. 1929	L	Everton	5–0
B. Butler	3	01. 01. 1930	L	Huddersfield Town	7–1
G. Gibson	3	15. 02. 1930	L	Leeds United	4–2
H. Blackmore	3	14. 03. 1931	L	Sheffield United	6–2
H. Blackmore	3	19. 09. 1931	L	Middlesbrough	4–2
B. Butler	3	21. 11. 1931	L	Blackburn Rovers	3–1
J. Milsom	3	26. 03. 1932	L	Sheffield United	3–1
J. Milsom	3	16. 04. 1932	L	Blackpool	3–0
J. Milsom	4	07. 05. 1932	L	Liverpool	8–1
J. Milsom	3	17. 12. 1932	L	Sheffield Wed	3–0
J. Milsom	3	06. 05. 1933	L	Leeds United	5–0
J. Milsom	3	25. 11. 1933	L	Port Vale	3–0
J. Milsom	4	30. 12. 1933	L	West Ham United	5–1
J. Milsom	3	31. 01. 1934	FAC	Brighton & Hove Albion	6–1
R. Westwood	4	06. 10. 1934	L	Barnsley	8–0
G.T. Taylor	3	22. 01. 1936	L	Everton	3–3
R. Westwood	3	30. 10. 1937	L	Chelsea	5–5
J. Calder	3	06. 11. 1937	L	West Bromwich Albion	4–2

Player	Goals	Date	Comp	Opponents	Score
R. Westwood	3	15. 01. 1938	L	Grimsby Town	3–1
J. Roberts	3	15. 10. 1938	L	Everton	4–2
W. Moir	4	30. 08. 1948	L	Aston Villa	4–2
M. Barrass	4	06. 11. 1948	L	Manchester City	5–1
W. Moir	4	27. 12. 1948	L	Sheffield United	6–1
W. Moir	3	12. 03. 1949	L	Middlesbrough	4–1
N. Lofthouse	3	19. 08. 1950	L	Charlton Athletic	3–4
J. Wheeler	3	03. 01. 1953	L	Blackpool	4–0
N. Lofthouse	3	18. 02. 1953	L	Middlesbrough	5–3
N. Lofthouse	3	03. 04. 1953	L	Sunderland	5–0
N. Lofthouse	3	25. 04. 1953	L	Newcastle United	3–2
H. Hassall	3	07. 11. 1953	L	Portsmouth	6–1
R. Parry	3	05. 02. 1955	L	Wolves	6–1
N. Lofthouse	3	03. 09. 1955	L	Arsenal	4–1
N. Lofthouse	4	10. 12. 1955	L	Birmingham City	6–0
N. Lofthouse	3	17. 12. 1955	L	Chelsea	4–0
N. Lofthouse	3	18. 08. 1956	L	Blackpool	4–1
D. Hennin	3	04. 04. 1958	L	Aston Villa	4–0
N. Lofthouse	3	31. 01. 1959	L	Luton Town	4–1
F. Hill	3	04. 03. 1959	L	Chelsea	6–0
N. Lofthouse	3	26. 10. 1960	LC	Grimsby Town	6–2
B. McAdams	3	03. 04. 1962	L	Aston Villa	3–0
F. Lee	3	22. 09. 1962	L	West Bromwich Albion	4–5
F. Hill	3	09. 03. 1963	L	Sheffield United	3–2
W. Davies	3	02. 09. 1964	L	Southampton	3–0
W. Davies	3	07. 09. 1964	L	Carlisle United	3–0
W. Davies	3	08. 10. 1966	L	Preston North End	4–2
F. Lee	3	25. 02. 1967	L	Preston North End	3–1
R. Greaves	3	31. 08. 1968	L	Sheffield United	4–2
J. Byrom	3	09. 08. 1969	L	Millwall	4–1
J. Byrom	3	13. 08. 1969	LC	Rochdale	6–3
T. Wharton	3	15. 08. 1970	L	Luton Town	4–2
R. Hunt	3	21. 11. 1970	L	Birmingham City	3–0
G. Jones	3	05. 10. 1971	LC	Manchester City	3–0
R. Greaves	3	11. 12. 1971	FAC	Rossendale United	4–1
S. Lee	3	16. 04. 1973	L	Halifax Town	3–0
J. Byrom	3	06. 01. 1974	FAC	Stoke City	3–2
B. Kidd	3	23. 08. 1980	L	Newcastle United	4–0
B. Kidd	3	01. 11. 1980	L	Cambridge United	6–1
T. Caldwell	5	10. 09. 1983	L	Walsall	8–1
T. Caldwell	3	22. 09. 1984	L	Plymouth Argyle	7–2
G. Oghani	3	20. 10. 1984	L	Preston North End	4–0
J. Thomas	3	30. 01. 1988	L	Peterborough United	4–0
J. Thomas	3	23. 04. 1988	L	Newport County	6–0
J. McGinlay	3	05. 03. 1994	L	Charlton Athletic	3–2
J. McGinlay	3	23. 04. 1994	L	Middlesbrough	4–1
J. McGinlay	3	27. 11. 1996	LC	Tottenham Hotspur	6–1

ACKNOWLEDGEMENTS

I would like to express my most sincere thanks to the following individuals and institutions who helped me in the compilation of this book.

Of great importance was Simon Marland (Bolton Wanderers' club accountant and historian) who kindly loaned me a wealth of photographic material for inclusion in the book, without which this publication would have been extremely difficult to produce. Thanks also to Dave Higson for the loan of material which included photographs and a letter from Kenneth Wolstenholme relating to his role as the Wanderers' match commentator.

A number of photographs were from the *Lancashire Evening Post* and my own private collection. Some are very early photographs and unfortunately of poor quality: I feel that they give the flavour of the period and hope that they will not detract from your enjoyment of the book.

After spending eight years as a primary school headteacher I am now earning my living as a freelance sports writer, and though I have had over 40 books published I can honestly say as a lifelong supporter of the Wanderers that this book has given me the greatest pleasure.